NATIVE NORTH AMERICAN ALMANAC

Wapiti regional library

NATIVE NORTH AMERICAN ALMANAC

Volume I

Cynthia Rose and Duane Champagne, Editors

An Imprint of Gale Research Inc.

NATIVE NORTH AMERICAN ALMANAC

Cynthia Rose and Duane Champagne, *Editors*

Staff

Sonia Benson, *U·X·L Associate Developmental Editor*
Thomas L. Romig, *U·X·L Publisher*

Keith Reed, *Permissions Associate (Pictures)*
Margaret A. Chamberlain, *Permissions Supervisor (Pictures)*

Mary Kelley, *Production Associate*
Evi Seoud, *Assistant Production Manager*
Mary Beth Trimper, *Production Director*

Mary Krzewinski, *Cover Designer*
Cynthia Baldwin, *Art Director*

The Graphix Group, *Typesetter*

™ This book is printed on acid-free paper that meets the minimum requirements of American National Standard for Information Sciences—Permanence Paper for Printed Library Materials, ANSI Z39.48-1984.

ISBN 0-8103-9820-6 (Set)
ISBN 0-8103-9814-1 (Volume 1)
ISBN 0-8103-9815-X (Volume 2)

Printed in the United States of America

Published simultaneously in the United Kingdom
by Gale Research International Limited
(An affiliated company of Gale Research Inc.)

I(T)P™

The trademark **ITP** is used under license.

READER'S GUIDE

Native North American Almanac features a comprehensive range of historical and current information on the life and culture of the Native peoples of the United States and Canada. Organized into 24 subject chapters, including major culture areas, activism, and religion, the volumes contain more than two hundred black-and-white photographs and maps, a glossary of terms used throughout the text, and a cumulative subject index.

Related reference sources:

Native North American Biography profiles 135 Native Americans, both living and deceased, prominent in their fields, ranging from civil rights to athletics, politics to literature, entertainment to science, religion to the military. A black-and-white portrait accompanies each entry, and a cumulative subject index lists all individuals by field of endeavor.

Native North American Chronology explores significant social, political, economic, cultural, and educational milestones in the history of the Native peoples of the United States and Canada. Arranged by year and then by month and day, the chronology spans from prehistory to modern times and contains more than 70 illustrations, extensive cross references, and a cumulative subject index.

Native North American Voices presents full or excerpted speeches, sermons, orations, poems, testimony, and other notable spoken works of Native Americans. Each entry is accompanied by an introduction and boxes explaining terms and events to which the speech alludes, as well as several pertinent illustrations.

Advisors

Special thanks are due for the invaluable comments and suggestions provided by U·X·L's Native North American books advisors:

Naomi Caldwell-Wood
President, American Indian
    Library Association

Victoria Gale
Librarian, Lodge Grass High School
Lodge Grass, Montana

Comments and Suggestions

We welcome your comments on *Native North American Almanac* as well as your suggestions for topics to be featured in future editions. Please write: Editors, *Native North American Almanac*, U·X·L, 835 Penobscot Bldg., Detroit, Michigan 48226-4094; call toll-free: 1-800-877-4253; or fax: 313-961-6348.

A NOTE ON TERMINOLOGY: IS *INDIAN* THE RIGHT NAME?

Throughout the *Native North American Almanac* a variety of terms are used for Native North Americans, such as *Indian, American Indian, Native, aboriginal,* and *First Nations.* The Native peoples of the Americas have the unfortunate distinction of having been given the wrong name by the Europeans who first arrived on the continent, mistakenly thinking they had arrived in India. The search for a single name, however, has not been entirely successful. In the United States, *Native American* has been used but has recently fallen out of favor with some groups, and *American Indian* is now preferred by some groups.

Canadians, too, have wrestled with this question of names, and many Native Canadians reject the appellation of *Indian.* Métis and Inuit in Canada will not answer to the name *Indian.* Similarly, in Alaska the Inuit, Yupik, and Aleut peoples consider themselves distinct from Indian peoples and do not wish to be called *Indian.* The Canadians have developed a range of terms such as *Native, aboriginal, First Nations,* and *First Peoples,* which in many ways more accurately describes the Native peoples.

Native peoples in North America do not form a single ethnic group and are better understood as thousands of distinct communities and cultures. Many Native peoples have distinct languages, religious beliefs, ceremonies, and social and political systems. No one word can characterize such diversity. The inclusive word *Indian* denotes the collection of people who occupied the North American continent, but it says little about the diversity and independence of the cultures.

The best way to characterize Native North Americans is by recognizing their specific tribal or community identities, such as Blackfeet, Cherokee, or Cree. Such identifications more accurately capture the unique and varied tribal and cultural distinctions found among Native North American peoples.

In compiling this book, every effort has been made to keep Native tribal and comunity identities distinct, but, by necessity, inclusive terminology is often used. We do not wish to offend anyone, but rather than favor one term for Native North American people, the editors have used a variety of terminology, trying always to use the most appropriate term in the particular context.

CONTENTS

Volume 1

CONTENTS

CONTENTS

Volume 2

PICTURE CREDITS

WORDS TO KNOW

A

aboriginal: native; the first or earliest group living in a particular area. When a group of people is called *aboriginal* it is generally being defined in contrast to colonizers or invaders of the land the group occupies. In Canada in the 1990s, the term *aboriginal* is commonly used to describe Native peoples.

aboriginal rights: privileges or claims that aboriginal people have, based on the fact that their ancestors were first to live in an area. Some examples of *aboriginal rights* are ownership of the land and its resources, the right to self-government, and the freedom to choose beliefs and cultural practices.

aboriginal title: the claim of the first inhabitants of an area to title or legal ownership of that area, based on the fact that they lived there first.

adjudicated: decided by a judgment, usually by a court of law.

AFN: See Assembly of First Nations

AIM: See American Indian Movement.

Alaska Native Claims Settlement Act (ANCSA): an act of Congress passed in 1971 that gave Alaska Natives 44 million acres of land and $962.5 million. In exchange, Alaska Natives gave up all claim to other lands in Alaska.

alienation: a feeling of being separated or withdrawn from society, from one's own identity, or from one's roots.

allotment: the practice of dividing up Indian reservations into privately owned parcels (pieces) of land. Tribes traditionally owned their lands in common, meaning that the tribe owned the land and all members could use and enjoy it. *Allotting* lands disrupted Indian societies greatly.

American Indian Movement (AIM): an activist organization founded by Native Americans in Minneapolis, Minnesota, during the 1960s.

annuities: money paid yearly to American Indians, according to the terms of treaties or agreements to give up lands. The U.S. government paid out *annuities* because it preferred to spread out the cost of payments over a period of years, rather than having to pay the money all at once.

ANCSA: See Alaska Native Claims Settlement Act.

archaeology: the study of prehistory; a scientific process of digging up and examining fossil relics, artifacts, and monuments of past human life.

Articles of Confederation: the original agreement made by the thirteen colonies in 1777 when they decided to form a new and independent country.

artifact: any item made by humans, such as tools or weapons, which is found by archaeologists or others who seek clues to the past.

Assembly of First Nations (AFN): the national organization that represents Indian nations to the Canadian government.

assimilate: to become like the dominant society (those in power, or in the majority).

B

band: Canadian term that originally meant a social and economic group of nomadic hunting peoples. Since Canada's confederation, however, the term also means any community of Indians registered under the Indian Act.

band council: in Canada, a form of Native government made up of a chief and council members who are responsible for conducting the band's business.

Berengia: the land bridge that existed over 15,000 years ago between present-day Siberia and Alaska.

BIA: See Bureau of Indian Affairs.

bilingual: speaking two languages fluently.

boarding school: a school where students live all or part of the year.

Bosque Redondo: the Navajo reservation in present-day New Mexico where the Navajo were forced to live between 1864 and 1868.

broadcast: to make public through radio or television.

Bureau of Indian Affairs (BIA): the U.S. government agency that oversees tribal lands, education, and other aspects of Indian life.

C

capitalism: a type of economy in which property and businesses are owned by individuals or group of individuals (rather than being owned by the government or by the society as a whole). Profits in a *capitalist* economy are based on competition and enrich the individual owner. Workers are paid a wage, or an agreed-upon amount, for their efforts.

census: an official count of the people in an area. A *census* is usually taken by the government, and includes information such as the number of people living in a house or apartment, their age, sex, occupation, and other facts.

ceremony: a special act or set of acts, performed by members of a group on special occasions, usually structured by the group's set of conventions and beliefs.

CERT: See Council of Energy Resource Tribes.

Civilized Tribes: See Five Civilized Tribes.

clan: a group of related families, which forms the basic social unit for some Indian societies.

comprehensive claim: in Canada, a land claim based on aboriginal rights to the land, where no treaties are involved.

collective good: the well-being of the group as a whole, usually resulting from the members working together cooperatively.

confederacy: a group of people, states, or nations joined together for a special purpose or mutual support.

conservation: protection and preservation of something; a carefully planned management system to prevent exploitation, destruction, or overuse.

conservative: traditional; wishing to preserve what is already established, such as traditions or political and economic structures.

convert: to cause a person or group to change their religious beliefs. A *convert* is a person who has been *converted* to a new belief.

cooperative: a type of business in which members share in the profits and losses; sometimes called a co-op. As the name implies, *cooperatives* are based on the cooperation of members; they aim to increase the wealth of the whole group, not just certain individuals.

Council of Energy Resource Tribes (CERT): an organization formed by tribes in the United States for the purpose of managing the natural resources on their reservations.

creation stories: sacred myths or stories that explain how the earth and its beings were created.

culture: the set of beliefs, social habits, and ways of surviving in the environment that are held by a particular social group. *Culture* is also the word for a group that shares these traits.

culture area: a region in which several tribes live and share similar cultures; their languages may or may not be similar.

curriculum: the courses or classes offered in a school.

D

Dawes General Allotment Act of 1887: a law that supported the U.S. government's practice of dividing up reservation lands into small parcels, which were given to individual tribe members.

demography: the study of populations, including information on migration, birth, death, health, and marriage.

displace; displacement: to remove a group from its usual place of residence.

diversity: variety; difference.

division of labor: dividing up, or sharing, different kinds of work among the people of a society.

drums: groups of Indian men singers (and recently women singers, too) often from different tribes, who get together to perform at powwows or other gatherings.

E

economy: the way a group obtains, produces, and distributes the goods it needs; the way it supports itself and accumulates its wealth.

economic development: the process of creating or improving a society's economy.

epidemic: the rapid spread of a disease so that many people in an area have it at the same time.

extinct: no longer existing. Many Indian tribes became *extinct* due to diseases brought by European explorers and settlers. Languages can become *extinct* when no one remains alive to remember or speak them, and they have not been written down.

F

First Nations: a term used for aboriginal peoples. The term *First Nations* began to be used in Canada in the 1970s.

Five Civilized Tribes: a name given to the Cherokee, Choctaw, Chickasaw, Creek, and Seminole during the mid-1800s. These tribes were so named because they had democratic governments, wrote constitutions, and ran schools in which the students could often read and write better than white children living nearby.

formal education: structured learning that takes place in a school or college, under the supervision of teachers.

G

gender role: the expectation within a social group of particular functions and behaviors from a person, based on whether that person is a male or a female.

general assistance: help, usually in the form of money, given by the government to people who are unable to support themselves.

Ghost Dance: a revitalization (renewal or rebirth) movement that arose in the 1870s. The *Ghost Dance* movement aimed to bring back to life traditional lifestyles, the buffalo, and many of the people killed by epidemic diseases.

Great Basin: an elevated region in the western United States in which all water drains toward the center. The *Great Basin* covers part of Nevada, California, Colorado, Utah, Oregon, and Wyoming.

guardian spirit: a sacred power, usually embodied in an animal such as a hawk, deer, or turtle, that reveals itself to an individual, offering help in important matters such as hunting or healing the sick.

H

harmony: a condition in which feelings, ideas, and actions all work together smoothly, or a state in which people work together in concert; the idea comes from music, when several notes played at the same time seem to fit together to make up one sound that is pleasing.

Haudenosaunee: the name of the people often called Iroquois or Five Nations. *Haudenosaunee* means "People of the Longhouse."

higher education: education at a college, university, or other post-secondary learning institution.

holistic: concerned with all the aspects of health, including the physical, mental, emotional, and spiritual. *Holistic* medicine heals the whole person—body, mind, and spirit.

I

image: in art, a picture or representation of something; for example, a warrior might dream of an eagle and then draw an *image* of the eagle on his teepee. In a social context an *image* is a mental picture or idea of someone or something held by a person or group. When Hollywood movies repeatedly portray Indians in a particular way, the American public may form an inaccurate *image* of what American Indians are like.

immunity: resistance to disease; the ability to be exposed to disease without necessarily getting it.

Indian Act: in Canada, the law that defines government policies toward Indians, first passed in 1876 and revised in 1985.

Indian country: reservations and sometimes nearby lands where Indian government and customs rule.

Indian Reorganization Act of 1934 (IRA): a law that ended allotment and gave tribes the option to form their own governments.

Indian Territory: the area of present-day Kansas and Oklahoma where the U.S. government once planned to move all Indians. In 1880, nearly one-third of all U.S. Indians lived there.

indigenous: native to an area.

informal education: learning that takes place outside of a school or classroom. Learning—through observation, participation, or practice—things like how to prepare for a ceremony, make a teepee, or speak a language.

interior: the part of a country or region that is away from the coast or border; inland.

Inuit: those aboriginal peoples who live north of the treeline in Alaska, Canada, and Greenland. The *Inuit* were formerly known as Eskimos. The word *Inuit* means people.

Inuk: singular form of Inuit.

IRA: See Indian Reorganization Act.

Iroquois Confederacy: an alliance formed by the Mohawk, Cayuga, Onondaga, Oneida, and Seneca, and later joined by the Tuscarora; also called League of the Iroquois, Five Nations, or Six Nations (after the Tuscarora joined).

K

Kachina: a group of spirits among the Pueblo; also refers to dolls made in the image of *Kachina* spirits.

kiva: among the Pueblo, a circular underground room used for ceremonies.

L

land runs: during the 1890s, spectacular one-day chances for non-Natives to get former Indian lands in Oklahoma .

language family: a group of languages that are different from one another but are related. These languages share similar words, sounds, or word structures. The languages are similar either because they have borrowed words from each other or because they originally came from the same *parent language*.

legal system: a group's laws, and the way they are learned and enforced.

legend: a story or folktale that tells about people or events in the distant past and is believed by many people.

life expectancy: the average number of years a person may expect to live.

literacy: the state of being able to read and write.

loan words: words that people who speak one language have taken or "borrowed" from another language.

Long Walk of the Navajo: the enforced 300-mile walk of the Navajo to Bosque Redondo in 1864.

longhouse: a large, long building in which several families live together; usually found among Northwest Coast and Iroquois peoples.

M

maize: corn. Maize was first grown in Mexico over 6,000 years ago.

Manifest Destiny: the belief held by many Americans during the 1840s that the United States should expand across the continent, and that fate determined that it should do so.

matrilineal: tracing family relations through the mother; in a *matrilineal* society, names and inheritances are passed down through the mother's side of the family.

media: sources, such as television, radio, theater, films, newspapers, magazines, and other printed matter, through which information, entertainment, and other popular forms of mass communication reach audiences.

Medicine Chest Clause: in Canada, a section of Treaty No. 6 (1876) which promised that the government would provide medical supplies to the Indians.

mercantile: having to do with trade or merchants (people who buy and sell in order to make a profit).

Métis: French word for "mixed-blood." This term has been used in different ways. Usually it refers to a specific group of people in western Canada. The Canadian Constitution recognizes *Métis* as aboriginal peoples. The term is also applied to any people descended from marriages between Europeans and Indians.

migration: movement from one place to another. The *migrations* of Native peoples were often done by the group, with whole nations moving from one area to another.

mission: an organized effort by a religious group to spread its beliefs in other parts of the world; *mission* refers either to the project of spreading a belief system or to the building(s) in which this takes place.

mission school: a school established by missionaries to teach people new religious beliefs, as well as other subjects.

myth: a story passed down through generations, often involving supernatural beings. *Myths* often express religious beliefs or the values of a people. They may attempt to explain how the earth and its beings were created, or why things are as they are.

N

neophyte: a new convert.

nomadic: traveling and relocating often, usually in search of food and other resources or a better climate.

non-recognized tribe: an Indian community that does not have official status with the U.S. government. Such a tribe may have been terminated by the government, or it may never have signed a treaty with the government.

non-status Indians: aboriginal people in Canada whom the government does not recognize officially as Indians under the Indian Act.

non-treaty Indians: aboriginal people whose status with the Canadian government does not involve any treaties.

Nunavut: a proposed new territory covering most of Canada north of the treeline, inhabited primarily by Inuit.

O

open access: a European concept of land use in the sixteenth and seventeenth centuries in which it was held that any area not legally owned by an individual or other legal party could be used for hunting or obtaining other resources without regard to traditional territorial control.

oral traditions: history, mythology, folklore, and other foundations of a culture that have been passed by spoken word, often in the form of stories, from generation to generation within a culture group.

oral literature: oral traditions that are written down after enjoying a long life in spoken form among a people.

P

pan-Indian, pan-tribal: taking into account all Indians regardless of tribes; *pan-Indian* groups often organize Native peoples from many tribes to work on issues that affect all Indians.

parent language: a language that is the common source of two or more languages that came into being at a later time.

passive resistance: going against a power or authority by means of not cooperating with them.

perspective: the viewpoint from which something is seen; the background or position from which a subject is mentally viewed or considered.

petroglyph: a carving or engraving on rock; a common form of ancient art.

peyote: a substance obtained from the button-like parts of the mescal cactus plant that some Indian groups use as part of their religious practices. By eating these buttons, which stimulate the nervous system, perceptions can be enhanced or altered during a ceremony.

pictograph: a simple picture representing a historical event.

policy: a statement in which a government tells how it will handle certain situations or people, or what its goals are.

population density: the number of people living in a given unit of area. The *population density* of New York City is very high because a lot of people live there in a small area. In contrast, the Mojave desert has a low *population density.*

potlatch: a feast or ceremony, commonly held among Northwest Coast groups; also called "giveaways." During a *potlatch,* goods are given away to show the host's generosity and wealth. Potlatches celebrate major life events such as birth, death, or marriage.

prehistory: a period of time in a given area when writing did not exist and there are therefore no written records to document the history of the era.

province: a district or division of a country. Canada is divided into ten *provinces* and two territories.

pueblo, Pueblo: pueblos are the many-storied stone or adobe Indian villages of the American Southwest. *Pueblo* is also the name that has been given to the Indian people who live in these villages.

R

rancheria: a small Indian reservation, usually in California.

ratify: to approve or confirm. In the United States, the Senate *ratified* treaties with the Indians.

Red Power: A term used to describe the Native American activism movement of the 1960s, in which people from many tribes came together to protest the injustices of American policies toward Native Americans.

Removal Act: an act passed by Congress in 1830 which directed that all Indians should be moved to Indian Territory, west of the Mississippi River.

Removal Period: the time, mostly between 1830 and 1860, when most Indians were removed from their homelands and relocated west of the Mississippi.

reservation: land set aside by the U.S. government for the use of groups of Indians.

reserve: In Canada, land set aside for specific Indian bands. *Reserve* means in Canada approximately what *reservation* means in the United States.

revitalization: the feeling or movement in which something seems to come back to life after having been quiet or inactive for a period of time.

ritual: a formal act that is performed in basically the same way each time; the acts that are performed in a ceremony or part of a ceremony.

rural: having to do with the country; opposite of urban.

S

sacrilege: the violation of what is sacred to a group.

self-determination: often means a person's right to choose his or her own way of life. The term also refers to the right of a group of people to choose and direct the way of life within their community, including the authority to make and enforce laws.

shaman: a person within certain Native American groups who understands supernatural matters. *Shamans* traditionally performed in rituals and were expected to cure the sick, envision the future, and help with hunting and other economic activities.

sister languages: languages that stem from a common source, the *parent language. Sister languages* usually differ from each other because they developed in a different area, but they retain some or many similarities.

smallpox: a very contagious disease which spread across North America and killed many thousands of Indians. Survivors had skin that was badly scarred.

sovereignty: self-rule; freedom from the rule or control of outside parties.

specific claim: in Canada, a claim by aboriginals based on rights given by treaty or legislation.

status Indians: in Canada, those aboriginals who meet the definition of Indian as determined by the Indian Act.

subsistence economy: a way of keeping alive by producing food and other goods for one's own use. In a *subsistence economy,* people may grow their own fruits and vegetables, raise livestock or hunt, and make their own clothing. *Subsistence* farmers use what they grow rather than selling it.

Sun Dance: a renewal and purification (cleansing) ceremony, performed among many Plains Indians such as the Sioux and Cheyenne.

sweat lodge: a sacred ceremony often conducted by a medicine man. A small dome-shaped lodge is built, and steam is created by pouring water on hot rocks. The *sweat lodge* is used for a variety of purposes, including spiritual healing.

sweetgrass ceremony: a ceremony in which sweetgrass is burned and participants rub the smoke on themselves—similar to the use of incense in other religions.

syllabary: a system of writing that uses characters (letters) to represent whole syllables (rather than letters representing consonants and vowels, as in an alphabet system).

symbol, symbolic meaning: a *symbol* is something that stands for or represents an idea, emotion, or any other concept; for example, to some cultures the eagle is a *symbol* of power and strength. A *symbolic meaning* is the idea that the symbol represents; for example, the *symbolic meaning* of the eagle is power and strength.

T

termination: the policy of the U.S. government during the 1950s and 1960s to end its trust relationship with Indian nations.

title: a statement or document that shows ownership of a piece of property. In the United States and Canada, one must have *title* to a piece of property in order to be recognized as the legal owner.

totem: an animal, bird, fish, plant, or other natural

object that a person or group takes as its emblem or protective spirit.

Trail of Tears: a series of forced marches in the 1830s caused by the U.S. government's removal policy. Cherokee, Creek, Seminole, and perhaps some Choctaw were moved from the Southeast to Indian Territory, causing the deaths of thousands.

travois: a hauling vehicle made of two long poles that bear a platform or net to carry loads. Before the Spanish brought horses to North America, many Native groups used dogs to pull the *travois.*

treaty: an agreement between two parties or two nations, signed by both, usually defining the benefits to both parties that will result from one side giving up title to a territory of land.

treaty Indians: in Canada, those Indians who are entitled to benefits under treaties signed between 1725 and 1921.

tribe: a group of Natives who share a name, language, culture, and ancestors; in Canada, called a band.

tribalism: loyalty to one's group.

Trickster: a common culture hero in Indian myth and legend. *Trickster* takes different forms among various groups; for example, Coyote in the Southwest, Ikhtomi Spider in the High Plains, and Jay or Wolverine in Canada.

trust: a relationship between two parties (or groups), in which one is responsible for acting in the other's best interests. The U.S. government has a *trust* relationship with tribal nations. Many tribes do not own their lands outright; according to treaty, the government owns the land "in trust" and tribes are given the use of it.

tundra: plains in arctic and subarctic regions that consist of a mucky soil on top of a permanently frozen subsoil. Plant life in the *tundra* is usually limited to mosses, lichen, and small shrubs.

U

unemployment rate: the percent of the population that is looking for work, but unable to find any. People who have quit looking for work are not included in *unemployment* figures.

urban: having to do with cities and towns.

urbanization: the process of moving from a rural to an urban environment, or from the country to the city. For many Native Americans, *urbanization* means moving from the reservation to a city or town.

V

values: the ideals that a community of people shares.

vision quest: a sacred ceremony in which a person (often a teenage boy) goes off alone and fasts, living without food or water for a period of days. During that time, he hopes to learn about his spiritual side and to have a vision of a guardian spirit who will give him help and strength.

visual arts: art forms that aim to please solely through the eye, as opposed to dramatic arts or literature, which also involve reading or listening. Examples of visual arts are painting, photography, sculpture, textiles, and pottery.

W

wampum: small cylinder-shaped beads cut from the shell of the quahog (a large clam found on the Atlantic coast). Long strings of *wampum* were used as money.

wampum belt: a broad woven belt of wampum, used to record history, treaties among the tribes, or treaties with colonists or governments.

weir: a barricade used to funnel fish toward people who wait to catch them.

NATIVE NORTH AMERICAN
ALMANAC

1

A Brief Overview of Native North American History

Early Immigration to European Contact

FACT FOCUS

- According to archaeologists, by 11,000 B.C. (some say as early as 18,000 B.C.) small bands of hunters crossed the Bering Sea Land Bridge from Siberia and passed into Alaska. These people and their descendants, who eventually spread throughout North and South America, are the ancestors of all later generations of Native Americans.
- At one time, there were more nations in North America than in all of Europe.
- Alaska's first pottery was produced in about 800 B.C. The style and method of making pottery indicates a possible contact with Asia around that time.
- Many groups in the East in about 1 A.D. were practicing a form of government based on the principles of modern-day democracy.
- The Anasazi, who emerged in the Southwest about 400 A.D., designed their communities in large multi-roomed apartment buildings—some with more than 1,200 rooms.

Archaeology and History

Native North American history dates back thousands of years before there were written documents. Although we cannot learn about ancient American history from memoirs, government records, essays, census polls, or any of the written material that later American history is drawn from, there are several ways we can come to understand aspects of what life was like in North America before the Europeans began recording what they observed on the continent in the sixteenth century. Two widely accepted sources of early American history are the science of **archaeology**—the study of the things previous societies left behind—and the **oral traditions** that have been passed down from generation to generation among Native American groups.

Archaeologists dig up the ruins of old societies, finding homes and other buildings, as well as tools, arts and crafts, and even remnants of foods eaten by ancient cultures. They can date these **artifacts** through scientific methods. (Some North American artifacts are thought to be 20,000 years old.) By analyzing the things people used in their daily lives, archaeologists can make informed judgments about the way people lived in past times.

Most Native American tribes have oral traditions about the past that explain their origins and history. These traditions are made up of a whole network of stories that a group tells about itself. Through these stories a great deal can be learned about the way that group of people perceived the world, and how it has remembered its own history.

Although writing as we know it did not exist in North America before the Europeans arrived, Native peoples had other ways of recording history. Some groups used **pictographs,** simple pictorial representations of historical events. Pictographs were created on animal hides and on teepees and other dwellings and etched into the rocks of cliffs and caves. Other groups used wampum belts, broad woven bead belts, to record treaties and other events.

WORDS TO KNOW

archaeology: the study of **prehistory;** a scientific process of digging up and examining fossil relics, artifacts, and monuments of past human life.

artifacts: objects that have been left behind by previous civilizations and cultures.

culture: the set of beliefs, social habits, and ways of surviving in the environment that are held by a particular social group. *Culture* is also the word for a group that shares these traits.

diversity: variety; difference.

oral traditions: history, mythology, folklore, and other foundations of a culture that have been passed by spoken word, often in the form of stories, from generation to generation within a culture group.

pictograph: a simple picture representing a historical event.

prehistory, prehistoric: a period of time in a given area when writing did not exist and there are therefore no written records to document the history of the era.

This chapter's approach to the history of North America before A.D. 1500 is based largely on archaeological discoveries. Through these discoveries, scientists and historians have pieced together a history of North American civilization that begins in the Ice Ages. This history tells us about outward patterns of different groups of people: how they obtained food, made tools, built houses, buried their dead, and generally survived in their environment. Much remains

Prehistoric pictographs on sand rocks, Adamana, Arizona.

unknown, and among archaeologists there are different interpretations of the story told by ancient artifacts.

11,000 B.C. to 8000 B.C.: The Paleo-Indian Age

Sometime around the year 11,000 B.C. (or according to some archaeologists, much earlier), small bands of hunters began to cross a land bridge that spanned the Bering Sea from Asia to Alaska. Groups probably kept crossing the bridge, called the Bering Sea Land Bridge, for many years. These first immigrants were the ancestors of all Native peoples of North and South America. Over many centuries they slowly moved southward, settling in what are now Canada, the United States, Central and South America, and the Caribbean islands.

The people who lived in North America from 11,000 B.C. to about 8000 B.C. are called the Paleo-Indians. The Paleo-Indians traveled in small groups, usually with a leader chosen by the tribe for bravery in hunting and war. They lived in caves, tents, or shelters that were temporary, so they could easily move on to a new home. They got their food by gathering wild plants and hunting animals such as mammoths (very large Ice Age elephants, now extinct), camels, and bison.

A wooly mammoth, one of the late Ice Age animals hunted by the Paleo-Indians.

Although Paleo-Indians did not have bows and arrows or advanced types of spears, some groups had very effective hunting practices. Bison herds were driven into gullies, surrounded, and then killed. Sometimes the Indians simply drove whole herds off cliffs. When the animals the Paleo-Indians hunted or the wild plants they gathered became scarce, the group simply moved on to a new territory, maybe just a few miles away.

Hunting and travel were done on foot; horses had disappeared from the continent not long after the first humans arrived. It is interesting to note, however, that dogs have been with humans from the first on this continent. Remains of dogs have been found in Paleo-Indian camps that date back to 10200 B.C.

Remains of Paleo-Indian hunting and gathering camps have been found all over North America. In the Arctic, nomadic groups survived the harsh environment by developing hunting techniques and tools suitable for the icy environment. Similarly, groups emerged and adapted to life in the Northeast, the Southeast, the Great Basin, the Great Plains, the Southwest, and the Northwest.

8000 B.C.: The Archaic Age Begins

Between 8000 B.C. and 7000 B.C. temperatures rose in North America, melting glaciers, forming rivers, and vastly changing the environment to something like its present state. Over many generations, people adapted to the changes within their local environment, marking the end of the Paleo-Indian period and the beginning of the Archaic Age.

With changes in the climate, food sources also began to change. People continued to

4

ICE AGE MAMMALS

The early human inhabitants of North America shared the continent with a very different group of animals than we know today. During the Ice Age many animals—the giant ground sloth, the woolly mammoth, and the dire wolf—became extinct. Because these animals had lived for thousands of years with no human beings on the continent, they probably did not have defenses they needed to protect themselves from the human predators (hunters) who began to populate the continent. Some archaeologists believe that certain Paleo-Indian hunting practices, as well as climate changes, were responsible for the extinction of many of the large Ice Age mammals.

hunt and gather, but groups developed their own habits and tools as was best suited to their region. As the population on the North American continent increased, groups learned to live within smaller areas. There was less interaction among groups, and **cultural** differences became apparent.

For example, in about 6000 B.C. in what is now southwest Texas, the Coahuiltecan people formed a distinct culture that lasted until the Europeans arrived in the sixteenth century. Coahuiltecan people lived in small bands. They fished in the Pecos and Rio Grande rivers, hunted rabbits with throwing sticks, and gathered plants. They did not develop agricultural systems because the climate was very dry.

In about 5500 B.C. a group of cultures emerged in southern California that archaeologists call the Encinatas tradition. These cultures based their economy on coastal resources such as shellfish. In an area near what is now San Diego, the Encinatas tradition lasted until about A.D. 1000. Bearing in mind that the United States is less than 250 years old, these were stable and enduring cultures.

In about 5000 B.C. hunting and gathering groups began to live in small camps in the Arctic. The Arctic is the northernmost region of North America, with its shores on the Arctic Ocean. It includes parts of Alaska, Canada, and much of Greenland. The hardy groups that inhabited the Arctic hunted caribou, elk, deer, and moose in plains called the tundra. These plains in the bitterly cold northern climate consist of a layer of muddy soil covering a permanently frozen subsoil. Only certain plant life, such as moss and some shrubs, can survive in the tundra. The people who lived in this region had to develop very special tools and techniques simply in order to survive.

From 4500 to 2500 B.C. people in northeastern California were the first known groups in North America to build sturdy earth lodges in permanent villages. In the later part of this period, however, the climate became more dry, and many groups of the region were forced to leave their homes.

In 2000 B.C. groups of hunters and fishers became the first humans to live in the eastern Arctic, one of the world's harshest

Two Inuit fishing in a traditional manner.

environments. These people were the ancestors of the modern Inuit (formerly called Eskimos). They developed remarkable technology—including special harpoons and other techniques for hunting seals, walrus, and whales—which made survival possible.

2500 B.C. to European Contact

Agriculture

The Archaic Age continued until 2500 B.C. and beyond. The end of the age was marked by the rise of agriculture (farming) in many areas. However, not all Indian groups changed from hunting and gathering to agri-

culture before European contact because, for many, there was no need to change. Their food was nutritious and plentiful, and their lives were relatively secure. In fact, from early times, many Indian groups worshipped the animals they hunted, making hunting not only a means of getting food, but also a very important part of their cultural and spiritual traditions.

The development of agricultural practices had a tremendous effect on the social patterns of many Native American groups. Hunters and gatherers tended to live in small bands that moved frequently and therefore did not form the kind of social and cultural patterns that more settled ways of life brought about. But when care was taken to plant a crop, a tribe would stay in one place to reap the harvest. As farming methods and tools developed, permanent communities with some form of government often followed.

Farming came to different areas at various times of history, depending on climate, trade, technology (tools), and the other food resources available. Farming native plants, including squash, sunflowers, marsh elder, and may grass, began in the East in about 2000 B.C. By 500 B.C. agricultural practices among southeastern groups caused a shift from previously nomadic (wandering, or living without a fixed place of residence) lifestyles to community life in small, permanent villages. Newly developing pottery-making skills allowed storage of foods. Flour was ground from the seeds of sunflowers, marsh elder, and may grass plants. By about A.D. 1, societies in what is now Kansas seem to have been regularly growing maize (a variety of corn initially cultivated in Mexico more than six thousand years ago) for food.

In about 350 B.C. beans and squash were introduced in the Southwest. By A.D. 100 maize had become a major crop there, as in the East. Although not as nutritionally complete as other plants, maize was a strong and productive crop. It was also easily stored. By the year 800 A.D. some communities had begun large-scale storage of food, necessitating some form of government to distribute food fairly among the people of the community.

By 900 A.D. southwestern farmers had developed a variety of irrigation systems, such as canals, dams, and various planting methods, to conserve the scarce rainfall in the region. Agriculture had become an advanced and effective food source for the dry region. But in the thirteenth century many groups left present-day New Mexico for the moister climates of the Texas and Oklahoma panhandles, where farming was easier.

Technology

The stone tools of the Paleo-Indian era were mainly connected with hunting bison and cleaning the meat. Spear points, axes, scrapers, and knives were skillfully crafted by the Paleo-Indians. Bison bones and hides also provided the material for many tools, clothes, and even dwellings.

Grinding tools were first used to grind wild roots and nuts. Later, with agriculture, their use became more widespread for grinding flour from grains. The mortar and pestle was in use in California by about 3000 B.C., and grinding slabs were in use in the Southwest at the same time.

Ground foods required a more leakproof storage system than basketry could provide. Pottery was a major technological advance in the preparation and storage of food and other resources. The first pottery north of Mexico was made in the Southeast in about 2500 B.C. Plant fibers were used to strengthen the simple ceramic vessels. The use of pottery spread rapidly throughout the continent. Alaska's first pottery came into use in about 800 B.C., but its source was not necessarily neighboring tribes. The style and methods of making pottery in Alaska at this time were similar to those of Asian peoples, revealing a possible recent contact with Asia.

Different cultures required special tools for their lifestyles. Cultures in the South-

A monolithic stone axe from Georgia engraved with symbols of the Southeastern Ceremonial Complex.

spear points and barbed points made of bone. They also used advanced spinning machinery to make cloth.

Trade among the tribes advanced the methods of tool-making and use, because groups that had settled in one region were no longer limited to the resources found within their area. There is evidence of long distance trade of copper and of stones used for tool-making as early as 2000 B.C. By 100 B.C. an advanced group of societies in the Midwest called the Hopewell societies was trading with other groups throughout a vast area extending from the Great Lakes in the north to the Gulf of Mexico in the south. Their products included conch shells, shark teeth, mica, lead, copper, and various kinds of stone.

Centuries later, in A.D. 400, the use of the bow and arrow spread rapidly throughout the continent. This was a major advance in hunting and warfare among many different Native American groups.

Housing and Communities

As people settled into regions, they developed agriculture, technology, and trade to adapt in their own special ways to their local environments. As a result, community life and social habits became more structured. In about 1400 B.C. people along the lower Mississippi River began to live in planned communities that some archaeologists consider the first chiefdoms (villages governed by one principal leader) north of Mexico.

In about 700 B.C. the Inuit people north of Hudson Bay in present-day Canada formed the Dorset culture. Dwellings used by the Dorset culture included skin tents, sod hous-

west, for example, developed such tools as nets and sandals. In California, from 2500 B.C. until about 500 B.C., cultures living in permanent villages developed stone smoking pipes, various types of baskets, grinding stones, and other instruments. At that time fishing traps were used in the rivers of the Northeast. From 2000 to 400 B.C., groups in the Northwest developed harpoons and other fishing equipment, including slate

es, and pit houses. In 500 B.C. groups in the Ohio River Valley region formed the Adena Culture, which was characterized by burial mounds and small villages made up of circular semi-permanent dwellings.

By 100 B.C. Hopewell societies centered in Ohio and Illinois were building massive earthen mounds for burial of their dead and probably for other religious purposes as well. The Hopewell were among the first groups in North America to determine an individual's status in society by the standing of the family he or she was born into, rather than on personal merits.

By A.D. 1 in many parts of the East, groups were forming complex social systems. Leaders of these groups often were granted their power by the decision of the group as a whole, similar to modern-day forms of democracy.

A.D. 1 to A.D. 400. The Hohokam, Mogollon, Patayan, and Anasazi Traditions of the Southwest.

By the year A.D. 1, small, permanent villages appeared in the Southwest, ending the region's nomadic hunting and gathering lifestyle. In the Sonoran Desert of south-central Arizona, the Hohokam cultural tradition emerged. The Hohokam were hunters and gatherers, but turned to agriculture and developed massive irrigation systems to water their fields. The Hohokam people were probably the ancestors of the modern Pima and Papago. This cultural tradition continued until after Europeans arrived.

In southern New Mexico, eastern Arizona, and parts of Mexico, the Mogollon people developed small villages of earth-covered houses. Later they built multisto-ried pueblos—small towns made up of stone or adobe (large earthen brick) buildings that often housed many families. The Mogollon people developed systems for farming in a dry climate. Some of the modern-day western Pueblo Indians are thought to descend from the Mogollon.

The Patayan tradition covered a vast region in Arizona. The Patayans were among the first pottery producers in the Southwest. Their homes were small and made of wood or stone. They were hunters and farmers, growing squash and corn.

A group called the Anasazi emerged in about A.D. 400 in the Four Corners region of present-day Arizona, New Mexico, Utah, and Colorado. The Anasazi eventually designed their communities in large multi-roomed apartment buildings, some with more than 1,200 rooms! They were farmers. The Anasazi were also skilled potters and were known for the black-on-white geometric designs on their pottery. In the Hopi language, *anasazi* means "ancient ones." The people of the modern-day pueblos of New Mexico and Arizona are descendants of the Anasazi.

The Mississippian Cultures of the East

From A.D. 700 to 900 the cultures of what is now the eastern United States began to transform into the complex societies of the Mississippian period. Farming practices, based on maize and other domestic crops, advanced dramatically within many groups. In fact, by A.D. 1100, the health of many Mississippian people declined. Their poor health was probably due to overreliance on starchy foods, particularly maize. Beans—a good nutritional complement to maize—did not come into use until A.D. 1300.

The town of Secota, in present-day North Carolina, was engraved by Theodore de Bry in the seventeenth century to illustrate the village life of peoples he met. This drawing gives an idea of the ways of life that developed throughout the Southeast and Midwest at the beginning of the Mississippian period.

By A.D. 450 the Mississippian people were building conical burial mounds and some of the first flat-top mounds in North America. The flat-top mounds were probably built beneath temples or the homes of important people in the village. In around A.D. 800, a group of Mississippian people lived near present-day Little Rock, Arkansas, on what is now called the Toltec site. This site consisted of ten mounds arranged around a plaza and enclosed by a two-meter high earth wall. It was the most complex settlement known in the Southeast at the time.

Many of the Mississippian groups formed elaborate social and political systems. Leadership was hereditary (passed on along family lines) and the villages developed into chiefdoms. The societies participated in long-distance trade and a widespread religion now called the Southeastern Ceremonial Complex.

Communities in the Great Plains

In the Great Plains in the ninth century, various cultures were developing in river valleys. These groups obtained food by farming, hunting bison, and gathering wild plants. In the northern and central Plains they built large, well-insulated earth lodges. In 880 A.D. a group of Caddoans in present-day Oklahoma built a series of large, square ceremonial buildings around a plaza, which is now called the Spiro Site. Over the next two hundred years these buildings were periodically destroyed and rebuilt in an elaborate ceremonial practice. The Spiro Site became a major ceremonial and trade center.

In 950 A.D. a group of people migrated from Minnesota and Iowa to the Great Plains, bringing with them an advanced knowledge of farming. They settled in what is now South Dakota, where they farmed maize, squash, and other crops that could survive the rough weather. By A.D. 1000 a Central Plains culture emerged in Kansas and Nebraska. The groups in the Central Plains culture settled along the major rivers, farming maize, beans, squash, tobacco, and sunflowers. They lived in multifamily, earth-covered houses.

Northeastern Groups

From A.D. 1000 to 1300 people along the St. Lawrence River Valley in New York and Ontario began to build small villages and farm maize, beans, and squash for the first time in this area. By the end of the period these people were constructing multifamily longhouses (long buildings that housed many families, usually associated with the Iroquois). Some of the longhouses were more than two hundred feet long—the distance from home plate to outfield of a baseball field. The villages were surrounded by walls and other fortifications, showing that warfare was probably an important fact of life. These people were the ancestors of the Iroquois.

Cultural Centers Built between 1000 and 1500

By the year 1000 A.D. there were many advanced cultures existing throughout the continent. The cultures had their own particular identities, languages, and lifestyles. Many interacted with other groups. Both friendly trade and warfare among groups were common.

An early colonial drawing of an Indian town in the Southeast.

Existing tribes of Native Americans can often trace their ancestry to the groups and cultural centers of the five-hundred-year era before Europeans arrived on the continent. Many cultural centers were in existence when the Europeans arrived, and many more were later found by archaeologists. All tell the story of a continent wealthy with civilizations of all kinds. A few of the cultural centers are listed below.

Chaco Canyon, New Mexico. Between 1040 and 1150, pueblos were flourishing in northern New Mexico's Chaco Canyon. Some pueblos had hundreds of rooms. The biggest pueblos included Pueblo Bonito and Chetro Ketl. The pueblos of Chaco Canyon were connected by an extensive road system that stretched many miles across the desert.

Cahokia Site, Missouri. By about 1100, the Mississippian culture had reached its

Pueblo Bonito at Chaco Canyon.

highest level of social complexity. The Mississippian cultural center, now known as the Cahokia site, was near present-day St. Louis, Missouri. There were more than one hundred mounds at Cahokia. One of these, Monks Mound, was the largest ancient construction north of Mexico. Ten thousand people lived in the town surrounding the mounds.

Awatovi Site, Arizona. Awatovi was called by the Hopi "Place of the Bow Clan People." Awatovi was thriving in 1175, with about 1,300 ground floor rooms. More than one thousand people lived there. Later, a two-story pueblo was added. In the sixteenth century, Catholic missionaries built a church there.

Moundville, Alabama. Moundville was one of the largest ceremonial centers of the Mississippian tradition in the East. In about 1350 it consisted of 20 mounds and a village. Moundville was probably the center of a chiefdom that included several other related communities.

By the end of the 1400s, countless Native American civilizations had arisen. Although some had disappeared, many of these civilizations had thrived for thousands of years. The groups that remained lived in teepees, quonsets, longhouses, A-frames, pueblos, and other types of dwellings. They farmed, hunted, and traded. They buried their dead in various ways and practiced many religions. Native North Americans were also gaining considerable knowledge about medicine and astronomy and developing a wide variety of music and art. It is estimated that between two and three hundred languages were spoken on the continent.

European Contact

When they began arriving in 1492, Europeans brought disastrous new diseases and war to the continent, wiping out many groups. Because of the widespread annihilation of Native Americans over the next four hundred years, we may never know the histories of many of the civilizations that had inhabited the continent for thousands of years before Europeans explorers and settlers arrived.

Native North American groups all experienced contact with Europeans at different times and in different ways. By the time Europeans began to settle in parts of the western United States and Canada, Native peoples on the east coast of the continent had already undergone a prolonged and devastating contact with the colonists. Native American peoples in different areas experienced different groups of Europeans: Spanish, British, French, Dutch, and Russians. The various Native cultures also had different ways of responding to newcomers.

Because of the **diversity** of Native peoples, students of Native American cultures cannot look upon all Native North Americans as one group with one history. One way to view the diverse Indian nations of this continent is to divide the continent into a set of "culture areas," a term that refers to the geographical areas in which several Native American nations lived (or live today) at once. Culture areas provide a means to view Native peoples throughout the continent without losing sight of the unique identities and experiences of each of the cultures. [See Major Culture Area chapters, 3-12.]

2

U.S. Native American Populations and Their Lands

A Demographic Study

FACT FOCUS

- Between 1500 and 1900, the number of Native Americans in the United States shrank from 15 million to only a quarter of a million.
- From 1900 until today, the Native American population has increased. In 1990, there were about two million Native Americans in the United States.
- In 1682 French traders built a trading post in Illinois, and 18,000 Indians of many different tribes came to live nearby.
- By the mid-1700s, Russians had trading posts along the Pacific coast as far south as present-day northern California.
- To settle a land claim in 1991, the U.S. government paid the Zuni tribe $1.67 per acre for the 15 million acres of land that had been taken from them illegally.
- Many of the Iroquois of New York State fought on the side of the British during the American Revolution.

"Why does not the Great Father put his red children on wheels, so he can move them as he will?"—Chief Spotted Tail, Sioux

A Note about the Information in This Chapter

This chapter describes the many changes that occurred in Native populations in the United States, mainly between 1500 and 1900. It is a view of the **demography** of Native Americans, which is a study of their population in terms of birth and death rates, migrations, and diseases. For the Native populations of North America, the arrival of Europeans, beginning in 1492, was what is

---

called a demographic catastrophe. **Epidemic** diseases brought by the newcomers killed millions, warfare killed many more, and entire Indian nations were forced to relocate to new lands far away and live in conditions that were harsh and restrictive.

The colonists' desire for trade, in which many Native people participated with enthusiasm, brought many changes to Native cultures. Some Native peoples relocated in search of fur-bearing animals for trade. Sometimes entire tribes moved in order to be closer to trading posts and the goods they had come to depend on.

The end result of disease, migration, trade, and war was a tremendous loss of Native American life and land. Much Native culture, language, and history was also destroyed in the process. Native Americans were a clear majority on the North American continent for many years after the Europeans arrived, and, had their populations not been so drastically affected for hundreds of years, might have continued to be. But between 1500 and 1900, Native Americans passed from being the dominant groups on the continent to become an impoverished minority. How this happened is the subject of this chapter.

The Impact of European Diseases: 1500-1900

The greatest demographic change in Indian populations came from diseases brought by the Europeans. By the time of his second voyage in 1493, Spanish explorer Christopher Columbus and his crews had begun delivering deadly diseases to unsuspecting Indians, as did the European explorers and settlers who followed. North Americans had never been exposed to the diseases that were common to the newcomers, such as smallpox, measles, scarlet fever, or influenza (the flu), and therefore had no immunity (natural defenses) to them. Because the viruses were so common in Europe, Europeans could be exposed to certain viruses without necessarily getting sick, or if they did get sick, they were less likely to die. They could also become carriers of the diseases without knowing it. When they passed the germs they had brought with them from their homes to the Native peoples of North America, it brought about unimaginable disaster in terms of loss of life.

Contagious diseases swept through Native American communities with great speed and force. Sometimes entire Native societies were so greatly reduced that the few remaining survivors simply moved in with another tribe. There were many tribes about whom we have no written records because disease wiped them out before Europeans had a chance to record information about them.

Between 1500 and 1900, about 60 million Indians in North and South America had been killed by epidemics. By 1900 Indians had lost 98 percent of their lands, and disease had played a significant role in this loss. Reduced in size and weakened by disease, Native Americans were in not strong enough to successfully defend themselves against the land-hungry new governments and their settlers.

By 1900 the U.S. Indian population had sunk to a low of 250,000 people. It is estimated that there were between seven and fifteen million people on the continent when Christopher Columbus arrived in 1492. The Native population began to rise again dur-

Indian burial ground. Artwork by Major O. Gross, 1849.

ing the 1900s, however, and today there are about two million Native Americans in the United States.

Population Changes in the Sixteenth Century

The Southeast

The Spanish were the first Europeans to contact Southeastern tribes in the early 1500s. From 1539 to 1543 Hernando de Soto's Spanish army ravaged the area, killing warriors, kidnapping women, and spreading disease. In fact, de Soto's men found villages that were already empty because of disease. Indians had probably gotten the diseases from previous Spanish explorers whose travels went unrecorded. Infected Native Americans and traders then spread the diseases from village to village.

Along with the devastating loss of lives, the diseases brought by the Spanish caused significant changes in Native cultures. The cultures of many Southeastern groups collapsed because of declining populations. The structured societies of the eight-hundred-year-old Mississippian culture, which had been organized around powerful chiefs and priests, gave way and were replaced by **egalitarian** societies (loosely organized groups who shared power). These groups remained in a state of flux for long periods of time because they were constantly taking in the survivors of other tribes. They are known today as the Cherokee, Catawba, Creek, and Choctaw.

The Northeast

French and English explorers gave smallpox and other fatal diseases to Indian communities extending from the St. Lawrence River to North Carolina. Smallpox, for example, seems to have been introduced in the South by the Spanish and in the North by the British. In the early 1500s there were reports of outbreaks of smallpox among the Timucuan in Florida and among the Chesapeake Bay people, such as the Powhatan, Pamunkey, and Mattaponi. The smallpox virus spread into present-day Pennsylvania, where the Susquehannock lost so many people to disease that by 1580 the entire nation was reduced to only one village. In 1585, one quarter of North Carolina's Indian population died from disease.

Disease was not the only factor in population changes. As Europeans settled along the coastal areas of present-day New England, Native people living in these areas were forced inland in search of new homelands. Often this resulted in a chain reaction of warfare among Native peoples, as groups **displaced** each other.

The Southwest

As disease spread and populations declined, communities were abandoned in the Southwest. As an example, between 1500 and 1650, the ten Hopi pueblos that existed on the Little Colorado River were completely emptied and abandoned. Several waves of epidemics, including plague and smallpox, had struck the area. The survivors **migrated** to join five Hopi pueblos at Black Mesa in present-day Arizona. The experience of the Hopi was typical of what happened to many pueblos, including the Piro, Tiwa, Jemez, and Towa.

The Seventeenth Century

The high rate of Native American death from disease continued during the 1600s. In the two hundred years between 1500 and 1700, Native populations in the Northeast, Southeast, and Southwest were reduced to a mere one-tenth of what they had been. By the 1600s Indians in the East were under great pressure to migrate because of the colonists' desire for their lands. Warfare, raids, and conflict were a common feature of this century. Indians in the Northeast, Southeast, and Southwest who attempted to stay in their own homelands were often forced to submit to the control of the colonists.

The Northeast

By the late 1600s, colonists outnumbered Indians in the Northeast. The Indians who remained often sold what was left of their lands in order to survive. Reduced to poverty, most Indians lived on the margins of colonial society.

The Powhatan

English colonists found the Powhatan confederacy in the area that is now Virginia. The Powhatan confederacy was a group of 27 tribes with a total population of more than ten thousand. The English invaded Powhatan territory in 1607, causing some deaths among the Powhatan and their neighbors.

From 1613 to 1617, the Powhatan suffered a plague that earlier had killed half of Florida's Native population and spread northward. (It killed so many Massachusetts Indians that the Puritans believed that God had sent the plague to clear the way for them to settle on former Indian lands.) At various times until 1646, the Powhatan rose up against the colonists, but they were ultimately defeated and lost their lands.

The Fur Trade

The fur trade involved Indians selling beaver, deer, and other skins to the Europeans in exchange for manufactured goods, especially guns, hoes, and hatchets. The Europeans wanted furs to sell in Europe for hats, leather, and coats. After a few years of trading with the Europeans, many Indian groups quit producing their own goods. Some groups came to depend on the fur trade to supply even their most basic needs, such as food.

By 1615 some nations, such as the Potawatomi, Ottawa, and Chippewa, migrated into the interior of the continent in search of good hunting areas. Because the European demand for fur was so high, many Indian tribes began to hunt for more animals, for longer periods of time than had previously been their custom. Groups that were especially involved in trade often depleted the supply of fur-bearing animals in their territory and were forced to move.

The French established a trade alliance with the Huron, an Iroquoian nation living on the Great Lakes. In effect, the Huron became the middlemen for the French, delivering and demanding payment for French goods from other Indian nations. Soon the

> ## WORDS TO KNOW
>
> **adjudicated:** decided by a judgement, usually by a court of law.
>
> **allotment:** the policy, peaking in the 1880s and 1890s, of subdividing Indian reservations into individual, privately owned parcels of land.
>
> **assimilate:** to become like the dominant society (those in power, or in the majority). In order to be *assimilated* into society, Native people were expected to give up their own customs, languages, and beliefs.
>
> **demography:** the study of a population or group of people, including its size in numbers, migrations (movements from place to place), diseases, birth rates, and death rates.
>
> **displace, displacement:** to remove from the usual place; causing a people to have to seek a new home, often because another group has moved into their homelands.

Huron had established a large network of trade. The Five Nations (an Iroquoian group in upstate New York) had a similar arrangement with the Dutch. The Five Nations attempted to make a trade alliance with the Huron, which could have prevented the trade wars that followed, but the French prevented these arrangements.

In 1649 the Five Nations initiated a series of intermittent wars, now known as the Beaver Wars, against the Susquehannock, Huron, Neutral Nation, Erie, Wyandotte (or Wyandot), and other French trading nations.

Indians Trading Furs, by C. W. Jefferys.

By 1650 the Huron trade empire was destroyed, and the Ottawa became the middlemen between Indian nations of the Great Lakes and the French. The Five Nations continued to war against other Indian nations, pushing the Chippewa, the Illinois Confederacy, and the Ottawa farther west. The Chippewa, in their move west, invaded Sioux territory in present-day Minnesota. After heavy fighting, the Sioux moved to the Plains in 1700, where they adopted the buffalo-hunting and horse-based culture that they have become known for.

The fur trade had far-reaching consequences to the peoples of the Northeast. Many tribes were displaced or destroyed by the Beaver Wars. Some simply abandoned their villages and set off in small groups to find fur-bearing animals. Sometimes tribes who had never lived near each other came together in large trading villages. For example, in 1682 French traders built a post at Starved Rock, Illinois. Nearly 18,000 Illinois, Miami, and Shawnee came to live nearby in order to trade more easily.

The Southeast

The Spanish first settled in St. Augustine, Florida, in 1565. But there was very little European settlement in the Southeast until the English settled Charles Town in present-day South Carolina in 1670. Spanish attempts at establishing **missions** in Florida soon failed because diseases killed the Indians.

In the mid-1660s, smallpox and yellow fever epidemics killed many Florida Indians. In 1658, a measles epidemic killed ten thousand Indians in Florida, and another smallpox epidemic between 1665 and 1667 killed many more. Despite language and culture differences, many tribes, their numbers greatly diminished, joined together.

The Slave Trade

Between 1670 and 1710, trade between Southeast Indians and the English involved the capture and sale of Indian slaves. The English, who wanted slaves for their plantations, gave guns and other goods to Indians who would go with them on slave raids to the interior Indian nations (those living farther inland). The Choctaw, once a large nation living in present-day Mississippi and Louisiana, were practically destroyed by slave raids during the 1680s and 1690s.

However, Indians did not make particu-

THE HORSE IN NORTH AMERICA

The modern horse is thought to have evolved in North America in the Ice Ages. At some time while the Bering Land Bridge spanned the distance from Siberia to Alaska, herds of horses are thought to have crossed from North America into Asia and Europe. Horses that remained in North America flourished for thousands of years, and the human inhabitants of the continent probably hunted them for food. But sometime between eight to ten thousand years ago, horses disappeared from the Americas. The reason for this is not known. In the sixteenth century Spanish explorers of Mexico and the Southwest brought horses back to their native continent. Some horses escaped captivity and lived in herds in the wild. Sometimes Indians captured these wild horses that had made their way north. But Indians also traded for horses, and some groups raided other communities and took their horses. The horse quickly became an important part of many Native cultures, vastly changing their ways of travel, hunting, and warfare.

WORDS TO KNOW

egalitarianism: a system of government that practices treating all members of a group as equals, with each group member having an equal say in the community's political or economic decisions.

epidemic: the rapid spread of a contagious disease so that many people in an area become ill with it at the same time.

migrate, migration: movement from one place to another. The *migrations* of Native peoples discussed in this chapter were done by the group, with whole nations moving from one area to another.

mission: an organized effort by a religious group to spread its beliefs in other parts of the world; *mission* refers either to the project or to the building in which it takes place.

larly good slaves. Knowing the land better than the English, they escaped easily. After 1700, the English began to take Indian slaves to the Caribbean islands where it was harder to escape. Then they began to import slaves from Africa to work the plantations.

The Plains

Life on the Plains was forever changed by the northward migration of the horse. Horses could travel far and fast, and tribes who had them could raid other tribes for food rather than growing it themselves. Tribes were forced to acquire horses in order to defend themselves, and to seek revenge.

With the arrival of horses, nations that had lived by farming soon turned to buffalo hunting and raiding. Warfare increased greatly.

The Plains Culture (also called the High Plains Culture) emerged. It featured warrior societies, group tribal hunts, and the Sun Dance, a sacrificial ceremony intended to promote the well-being of the community. Although the western movie image of leather-clad Indians racing across the Plains on horseback has become one of the most widely known images of Indians in American culture, the Plains culture did not last long and was not typical of most Indian cultures.

In the north, farming peoples were moving onto the Plains. To the south, Apache and Navajo were moving in. The Apache and Navajo were hunter-gatherers, seeking big game and wild foods. They used pack dogs with travois (small sleds) to carry trade goods. Acquiring horses from the Spanish, they soon dominated the southern Plains.

The Apache and Navajo rustled (stole) Pueblo and Spanish livestock and traded slaves for other goods. Some Navajo acquired sheep, which they learned to pasture and breed. With a steady supply of mutton, the Navajo population began to increase. Today the Navajo are the largest Indian nation in the United States, with about 175,000 people.

The Southwest

Later in the 1600s the Apache also traded and raided in the Southwest. After disease killed many of their horses in 1670, they moved into New Mexico. There they depended on hunting and fighting for their survival. By 1698 some Apache had migrated west and settled on the present-day Arizona/New Mexico border.

In 1680, Pueblo peoples rose up and forced many Spanish colonists from their lands. The Spaniards, along with some Pueblo who were loyal to them, temporarily moved south to present-day El Paso, Texas, where their descendants still live today. But the Spanish returned to present-day New Mexico and reestablished rule there for many more years.

The Eighteenth Century

Epidemic diseases continued to attack Native communities in the 1700s, but conflict over trade and land became a more primary source of disruption to Native societies. The competition for Indian trade among Spain, France, and England affected nearly all Native American societies by the end of the 1700s.

In the East there was almost constant warfare, including Queen Anne's War, King William's War, the French and Indian War, and the American War for Independence. Indian nations with trade alliances with one of the European powers often found themselves fighting as allies to that power.

In the Southeast slave raids continued, causing many groups to relocate. Wars were fought over trade issues among the colonists and the Indians.

During the 1700s, several Native American groups chose to migrate in order to avoid the settlers' aggression and to keep their independence. After the Revolutionary War, many Iroquois moved to Canada to live on lands given them by the British as a reward for their loyalty during the war. Creek Indians moved into Florida and formed a new tribal group called the Seminole. Good-sized groups of Delaware, Shawnee, and others migrated into Missouri and Arkansas.

Union Pacific Railroad construction. Cheyenne Indians hunting buffalo near the newly laid tracks and telegraph lines.

Choctaw, Tunica, Biloxi, and others began to settle in parts of Louisiana and east Texas.

The migration of Native American groups to the Great Plains was probably the most significant movement of the 1700s. Before the introduction of the horse, Plains peoples grew corn and settled in villages in which houses looked like earthen mounds. Soon the Sioux and Cheyenne abandoned farming and adopted the High Plains Culture that featured the Sun Dance, buffalo hunting, and riding horses.

Other farming cultures, such as the Hidatsa, Arikara, and Crow, migrated north and settled in present-day North Dakota.

Kiowa and Comanche moved into the southern Plains from the Rocky Mountains.

During the 1700s, Russian, British, and American traders began to contact Native groups in Alaska and the Pacific Northwest. Seal and sea otter skins and other furs were in great demand and brought Native peoples in these areas into trade.

In California, the Spanish began to establish a system of missions reaching into the northern areas of the state. Thousands of Indians were brought into the missions as forced labor. Disease and poor living conditions killed many.

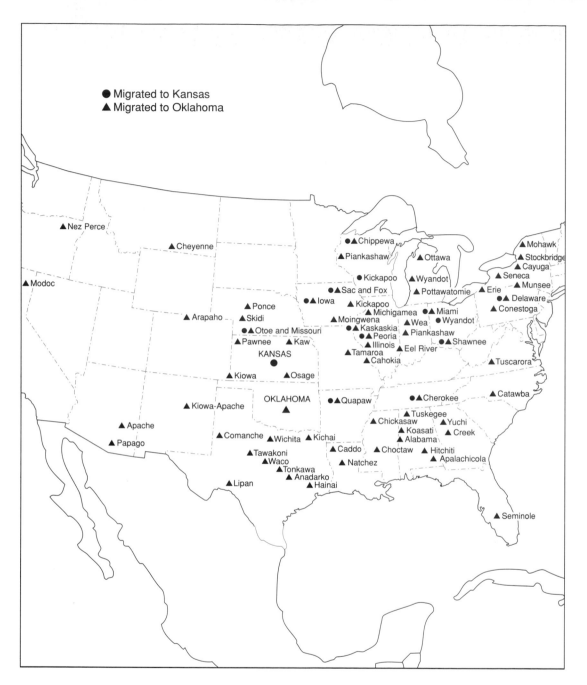

Homelands of Indians who were forced to migrate to Indian Territory in present-day Kansas and Oklahoma.

The Nineteenth Century

Manifest Destiny

A central goal of the United States during the nineteenth century was to fulfill its "Manifest Destiny." Manifest Destiny was the idea that the new nation was specially fated—or chosen by God—to expand all the way across the continent to the Pacific Ocean. Although by English and American law Native Americans had the natural and legal right to the lands they occupied, in their quest for one great nation spanning the continent, many Americans began to view Indians as an obstacle to the success of Manifest Destiny.

The United States Acquires Native Lands

The U.S. government was determined to acquire Indian lands. The principal way the United States obtained Indian land was through treaties in which Indians gave up large areas of valuable land for reservations and the promise of government protection and help.

Traditionally, most Indian cultures viewed the land as a resource to be shared, rather than to be bought and sold. Tribes generally held their lands in common, rather than dividing them up into privately owned plots. When treaties permanently took land away from them, many Native American groups found that the government had bought their lands through secret arrangements with one or two members of the group. Since the land was basically owned by all members of the group, these sales were an outrage to members who did not participate in the sale.

Indians Are Removed to the West

During the 1800s, the U.S. government wanted to remove all Indians east of the Mississippi River from their homelands and resettle them west of the Mississippi. Most of the treaties Indians signed with the government between 1817 and 1849 featured their removal to the so-called "vacant" lands in the West.

Removal did not happen all at once. Some tribes, like the Delaware, were moved several times. In 1680 the Delaware lived on the Atlantic Coast. By 1800 they were living in Indiana and Missouri. From those states they were moved four more times to Arkansas, then Texas, Kansas, and finally to Oklahoma.

"Indian Territory" and the Trail of Tears

A special territory called "Indian Territory" was set aside for the Indians. Originally it included Nebraska and Kansas, but was eventually reduced in size to what is now the state of Oklahoma.

The first Indians to be moved to Oklahoma were the Five Civilized Tribes of the Southeast—the Cherokee, Creek, Chickasaw, Choctaw, and Seminole. Poorly clothed and fed, they were forced to march over eight hundred miles during winter months. Thousands of men, women, and children died. This journey came to be known as the "Trail of Tears." Two of the tribes—the Creek and Seminole—fought back, but eventually they were removed also. By the end of the 1830s, the Southeast had lost from 60 to 90 percent of its Native population.

The Long Walk of the Navajo

Another example of forced removal was the Long Walk of the Navajo in 1864. The Navajo were angry over losing part of their

A general view of the Laguna Pueblo, New Mexico, 1879.

land through a treaty signed in 1858. Two years later, they attacked Fort Defiance, located in the middle of their territory. They were defeated and forced to march eight hundred miles to a 40-square mile reserve at Fort Sumner, New Mexico. Many died along the way. The nine thousand survivors found themselves on land that lacked water and had poor soil. The nearest available wood was 5 to 18 miles away. Hordes of grasshoppers swept the area.

On this land, the Navajo were expected to become farmers! The U.S. government did little to help the Navajo until a Santa Fe newspaper wrote about the terrible conditions on the reserve. As a result, the government allowed the Navajo to return to a small portion (10 percent) of their original home-

land. In later years more land was added as the Navajo population grew.

The Osage and Pueblo: Happier Endings

Like many nations in the 1800s, the Osage lost their homeland in Kansas in a series of treaties, and then lost over 50 percent of their people because of removal. Unlike other groups, however, when they arrived on their new land in Oklahoma, they discovered it was covered with excellent grass for grazing cattle. And below the surface was oil!

The Osage insisted on keeping the mineral rights for the tribe as whole—a tactic that protected their rights and provided an excellent source of income. Over a period of 40 years, their mineral rights earned the Osage roughly $300 million.

The Pueblo Indians in New Mexico and Arizona also fared better than most Indian peoples at this time. They already had full Mexican citizenship while under Spanish rule. When the United States acquired Pueblo territory from the Spanish in 1848, the Pueblo automatically became U.S. citizens. Although citizenship caused problems for the Pueblo in terms of getting protection as an Indian nation, the United States respected the Pueblos' right to the lands the Spanish had given them. They remained in their homelands.

U.S. Government Policies and Loss of Indian Lands

Assimilation

To support its goal of acquiring Indian lands, the U.S. government began a policy of **assimilating** Indians into mainstream society. In other words, they wanted Native people to give up their own ways of life and to blend in with the rest of American society. Part of the reason for this policy may have been a genuine belief that assimilated Native Americans would find equal treatment and receive a fairer share of the nation's wealth if they were not isolated from the mainstream. But the policy of assimilation was also supported by racism (the belief that, because of racial differences, a group of people is inferior to one's own group). Because many Americans had little understanding of American Indian cultural traditions, they simply perceived them as inferior to white ways. Racist attitudes were used to justify forcing the Indians to give up their lifestyles, beliefs, and land.

Many Americans, who were busy building a commercial society centered around industry and agricultural production, felt that Indians "wasted" land by hunting and trading over large areas. The government hoped that if Indians could be trained to farm small areas of land, they would no longer need so much land. If they didn't need as much land to live off, then they would be more willing to sell it to the United States.

Assimilation was not simply a matter of economics, however. Missionaries were hired to teach school, religion, farming, and homemaking to the Indians. These efforts to impose value systems and life styles upon people were not as successful as the government wished.

Allotment

By the 1870s, the United States was straining to find new ways to obtain Indian lands. Between 1853 and 1857, Indians had signed 60 treaties. Many of these treaties called for the **allotment** of tribal lands (meaning the land would be parceled out to individuals). To support allotment, the Dawes General Allotment Act was passed in 1887. Under allotment, tribes would no longer own their lands in common (as a group) in the traditional way. Allotment meant that land would be assigned to individuals. The head of a family would receive 160 acres, and other family members would get smaller pieces of land.

From the point of view of most Native Americans, the main problem with allotment was that it took away Indian control of their lives and lands. Many Indians could not make a living off the parcels of land they had been given. They had not chosen the way of life that they were forced into. Many Indians sold their lands as soon as possible,

Charles A. Bates, allotment officer on the Pine Ridge Reservation, with American Horse and an interpreter, about 1907.

in order to get money for survival. In many cases, whites bought Indian lands illegally and the government did little or nothing to stop them.

Allotment, along with conversion to Christianity and farming, was supposed to bring Indians into the mainstream of American life. Instead, these policies impoverished most Native American groups. Even today, Native people continue struggling to overcome the conditions created by government policies of the 1800s.

The Twentieth Century

The Myth of the "Vanishing American"

In 1900, when the Native American population in the United States had shrunk to less than 237,000 people, no one realized that the low point in Indian populations had been reached and that the number of Indians would increase greatly over the next century. By 1990, there would be almost two million Native American people in the United States. However, the destruction of Native people

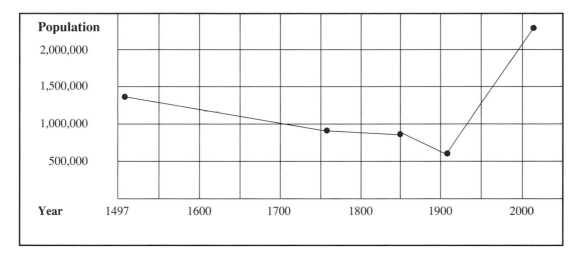

U.S. Native Population Trends, 1497-1990.

and their culture over the previous four hundred years gave rise to the idea that they were a "vanishing" or "dying" race. Often this idea was used to justify taking away Native lands and moving the people to places far away.

Government Policy in the Early 1900s

From 1900 to 1934, Indians were confined to reservations and continued to lose their lands through the process of allotment. Realizing how destructive allotment was to the Indians, Congress passed the Indian Reorganization Act (IRA) in 1934. The IRA ended allotment and restored some lands to the tribes. The IRA also encouraged tribes to govern themselves. Even so, tribal governments did not gain enough power over their money and lands to become truly self-governing and often found the government overruling their decisions.

Native Americans Claim Their Lost Lands

Before Columbus, Native Americans roamed freely over nearly three billion acres of land. By 1934, they owned only 48 million acres, and a great deal of this was uninhabitable desert land. Native peoples had lost over 98 percent of their lands!

During the twentieth century, tribes filed claims against the government for the unfair loss of their lands. Some were successful, others were not. Many land claims have lingered in the courts for years, even decades.

Congress Acts to Restore Some Lands

At various times, Congress has acted to restore some former lands or to add land to reservations. Some lands have also been restored as a result of land claims being pursued in the courts. The Havasupai, Yakima, and Taos and Zuni Pueblo were successful in land claim suits. Other tribes, like the Navajo and Hopi, did not succeed. Congress has also given a few eastern tribes money to buy land. For example, the Penobscot and Passamaquoddy in Maine were able to purchase about three hundred thousand acres of forest lands.

Navajo papoose on a cradleboard with a lamb approaching.

Land Claims under the Indian Claims Commission

In 1946 the Indian Claims Commission (ICC) was created. Its purpose was to decide land claims filed by Indian nations. Many tribes expected the ICC to return lost lands, but the ICC chose to award money instead. This angered Native Americans, particularly in light of the ICC's policy of awarding money based on the value of the land at the time it was lost. Often this was not more than $1.25 per acre!

Many Indians rejected this claims process along with the money that it offered. The Oglala Sioux, for example, continue to refuse an award of over $100 million for the Black Hills in South Dakota.

The ICC ceased to exist in 1978, and claims are now heard by the U.S. Claims Court.

Reservation Economics Today

Life on reservations has always been hard. Often the reservations are isolated in rural areas and residents have little or no access to services that most Americans take for granted. A considerable number of Indian families live at or below the poverty level and cannot survive without welfare.

On many reservations, job opportunities are limited. Unemployment can run as high as 50 percent. Most reservations do not have enough resources to comfortably support the residents.

Non-Indians frequently live on reservations. In Arizona, the Dakotas, and New Mexico the population is over 90 percent Indian. But in California, some of the Great Lakes states, and Washington less than 30 percent of the people living on reservations are of Indian heritage.

Nevertheless, many tribes have developed their lands and resources to provide a higher standard of living for their people. Tribal councils strive for more self-determination and have taken increasing control of community resources and programs. Native people are better educated today than ever before. Developing businesses and jobs remains a high priority on many reservations.

Urbanization

One notable trend among Native Americans in the twentieth century is to move away from reservations to towns and cities. Moving off the reservation is called urban-

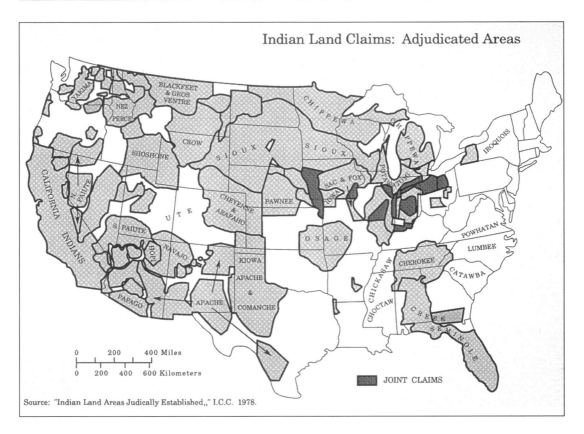

Indian Land Claims: Adjudicated Areas

JOINT CLAIMS

0   200   400 Miles

0   200   400   600 Kilometers

Source: "Indian Land Areas Judically Established,," I.C.C. 1978.

This map is based on "Indian Land Areas Judicially Established," as published by permission of the University of New Mexico.

ization. In 1990, 62 percent of all Indians lived in towns and cities, and more move to cities every day. Cities like Los Angeles, Oklahoma City, Phoenix, and Tulsa all have large Native American populations.

Unfortunately, moving away from the reservations does not always mean leaving poverty behind. For many Native Americans a move to the city simply means exchanging rural poverty for urban poverty. Poor housing, unemployment, and discrimination face urban Indians as well as those on reservations.

3

Native Groups of the Northeast

With an Introduction to the Study of
Major Culture Areas

FACT FOCUS

- Because of European epidemics and warfare, many of the nations that once lived in the Northeast disappeared before information about them could be recorded.
- Some Puritans viewed the widespread death from epidemic diseases they brought to Native Americans as an act of God, to clear the land for the Puritans' use.
- The Five Nations of the Iroquois was a confederation of nations dating back to around the year 1000. The Iroquois confederacy was used as a model for the United States Constitution.
- America's founding fathers invited Iroquois leaders to debates on the Declaration of Independence in 1776.

An Introduction to the Study of Major Culture Areas

Because there are many Indian nations in North America, people who study Native American **cultures** have divided the continent into a set of "culture areas," a term that refers to the geographical areas in which several Native American nations lived (or live today) at once. Within a culture area, the nations usually spoke different languages, practiced different religions, and adapted in different ways to their environment. But at the same time, the various cultures within one area responded to the same basic environment and to similar historical events.

For example, the Northwest Coast culture area includes groups such as the Tlingit in present-day Alaska, the Coast Salish in British Columbia and Washington, the Chinook in Washington and Oregon, and various Athapaskan and Penutian-speaking tribes in Oregon. Although throughout history these groups had their own languages and cultural traits, they all lived in an area with bountiful supplies of salmon and other seafoods. Many of their customs centered

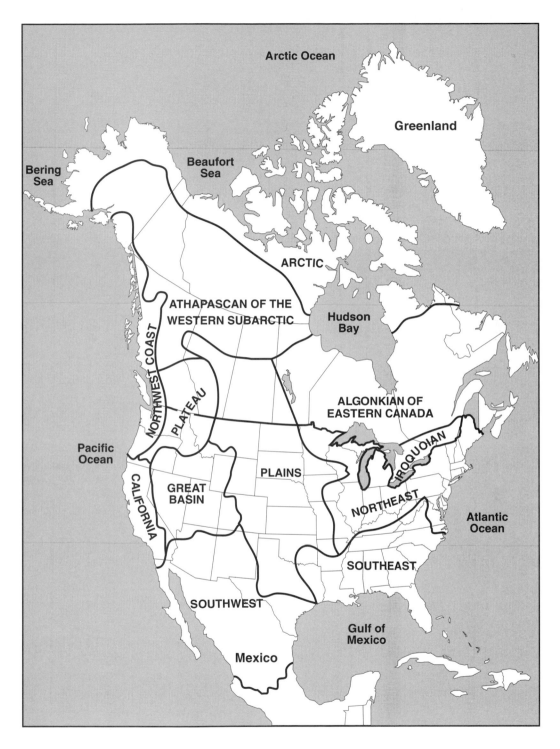

Major Culture Areas of North America.

on these resources. The groups in this area did not experience continuous contact with Europeans until the late 1700s, when the Northwest Coast groups first met with the Spanish, then the Russians. As trade developed in the area, bringing in more and more Europeans, disease became widespread. The various Northwest Coast groups, their own numbers diminishing and their economies vastly altered by trade, were rapidly outnumbered by non-natives. Although the area's groups faced similar environmental and historical events, each had its own way of coping and its own distinct history.

In the following chapters, nine major U.S. culture areas and the culture groups of Canada are described, including overviews of the history, culture, and contemporary issues of each area, as well as overviews of selected Native groups within the regions. The nine U.S. culture areas discussed in these chapters are: 1) the Northeast; 2) the Southeast; 3) the Southwest; 4) the Northern Plains; 5) the Northwest Coast; 6) Alaska; 7) Oklahoma; 8) the Plateau, Great Basin, and Rocky Mountains; and 9) California. Canada's culture areas are discussed in the chapter that follows, although for some culture groups, traditional homelands exist in both Canada and the United States.

Culture Groups of the Northeastern United States: An Overview

From 1000 B.C. to 1600 A.D. a variety of "mound-building" cultures was found in the Northeast. These cultures are now grouped together under three names: the Adena culture (1000 B.C. to 200 A.D.); the Hopewell culture (300 A.D. to 700 A.D.); and the Mis-

The Northeast (shaded).

sissippian culture (800 A.D. to 1600 A.D.). The mounds built by these groups were erected for religious reasons, often as burial memorials or as temples for spiritual leaders. The people within these cultures generally lived in villages, and corn was a staple of their diet. When Europeans arrived in the early 1500s, most Northeastern groups were living in fortified (protected) towns, with houses arranged according to clans (family lines). Northeastern peoples hunted, and some engaged in farming.

During the late 1500s, many Algonkian-speaking nations, such as the Delaware (or Lenape) and Wampanoag, lived along the coast of present-day New England. They lived by hunting, fishing, and growing corn, beans, pumpkins, and other vegetables. Other Algonkian-speaking nations, like the Ottawa and Ojibway, were moving into the Northeast. Iroquoian peoples occupied present-day upstate New York and sites along the lower Great Lakes.

Even before Europeans arrived, the population of the Northeast was shifting due to relations between its original tribes and newcomers to the area. In the 1500s Iroquoian peoples were being invaded by Algonkian groups. The arrival of Europeans in the 1500s heightened these struggles. Many groups were pressured to move farther and farther west as Europeans **displaced** Native communities. Those Native groups who relocated in turn displaced other tribes.

By the 1700s, many Northeastern tribes had moved into the Great Lakes region. These included the Ojibway, Potawatomi, and Ottawa. They displaced the peoples of the Illinois Confederacy, who moved from present-day Wisconsin into Illinois. Also during the 1700s, the Ojibway moved into the Minnesota region and began to compete for food resources, such as game and wild rice.

From 1497 onward, Indians of the Northeast were in almost continual contact with Europeans. The Europeans brought epidemic diseases to North America, killing thousands of Native people. Warfare and demands for land caused coastal groups to move inland. With their numbers already reduced by disease, these groups often joined other tribes or simply disappeared as distinct cultures. As a result, there may have been many Native communities in the Northeast United States that we know nothing about, because they disappeared before Europeans recorded information about them.

English Settlements and Warfare in the Northeast

The Native Americans of the Northeast, particularly those groups that lived along

---

WORDS TO KNOW

culture: the way of life of a given people or nation, including customs, arts, beliefs, social relations, and survival methods and tools.

displace, displacement: to remove from the usual place; causing a people to have to seek a new home, often because another group has moved into their homelands.

longhouses: very long buildings, usually associated with the Iroquois and their ancestors, that served as homes for a number of families and as places for worship and community gatherings.

matrilineal: tracing family relations through the mother; in a *matrilineal* society, names and inheritances are passed down through the mother's side of the family.

wampum, wampum belts: *Wampum* were small blue and white beads cut from the shell of the quahog, a large Atlantic coast clam. Long strings of *wampum* were used like money in trade. Broad, woven "belts" of *wampum* were used to record treaties among the tribes and, later, with Europeans.

---

the coastline, were generally quite receptive to the European newcomers as they first arrived to establish colonies in the 1600s. Unsuspecting of the disasters to come, Native groups in present-day New England and Virginia helped the English settlers through their first rough winters on the continent. Before long, the Native communities were stricken with deadly epidemics brought from Europe. Indians lost their lives to disease and warfare with the settlers, and, eventually, they lost their lands as well.

The Pilgrims arrived at Plymouth, Massachusetts, in 1620 and would probably have perished in their first winter if not for the help of Indians. The Wampanoag showed the Pilgrims how to hunt and fish and how to grow and prepare native crops.

The Puritans arrived in Massachusetts ten years later. Puritan philosophy proved to be extremely harsh toward Native Americans. Puritans believed that they were on a mission from God to establish a perfect Christian society. Puritan minister Cotton Mather called Indians the "accursed seed of Canaan" and preached that they should be made subject to Christian rule. Mather viewed the smallpox epidemic that killed thousands of Indians as a "remarkable and terrible stroke of God upon the natives." Some Puritans believed, along with Mather, that God had sent the diseases that wiped out the majority of the Native American population in the Northeast in order to clear the lands so that they themselves could settle there.

The Pequot, a tribe known for its war-like ways and disliked by many Indian tribes, lived in what is now Connecticut when the Puritans arrived. In 1634, Indians (probably the neighboring Narragansett) killed some Puritans that were hunting for Indian slaves. In retaliation, Puritans claimed absolute rule over the Pequot and demanded Pequot land and the surrender of the killers. The Pequot agreed to these terms. Two years later another Puritan was killed by Indians and the English again demanded the surrender of the

killer. This time the Pequot refused and war erupted. The settlers raised an army consisting of Puritans, Pilgrims, Mohican, and Narragansetts. The army attacked and set fire to the Pequot fort, killing as many as seven hundred Pequot men, women, and children.

After this the Puritans began to set up reservations for Natives. By 1671 there were 14 reservations in the Northeast that restricted Indian rights and forced them off their lands. Wampanoag leader Metacom, known to the English as King Philip, tried to put a stop to English settlers' tyranny by gathering an army from many area tribes. The army of Abenaki, Nipmuck, Narragansett, and Wampanoag Indians attacked more than half the English settlements in New England. Weakened by major epidemics, even the allied Indian forces were not strong enough to win the war, although they held their own against Puritan forces for a time. The Puritan government executed Metacom. His wife, son, and hundreds of his followers were sold into slavery. Many of Metacom's allies fled. By the end of King Philip's War (1675-76), the few remaining Indians in the New England colonies were living in small towns and had adopted Christianity. The colonists called these groups "Praying Indians," and their towns were often called "Praying Towns."

A similar fate had befallen the Indians of Virginia. The Powhatan Confederacy had saved the Jamestown settlers during their first winter in North America by providing them with food. The hostility of the settlers and their desire for land provoked the Confederacy into war after the group had tried for years to be good neighbors to the English newcomers. Warfare between settlers and the Powhatan Confederacy went on for

Tribal Territories in the Northeast.

many decades. But by 1675 the Powhatan Confederacy was demolished by Virginia settlers, and the Indians were forced to live under Virginia law.

Several northern groups, like the Penobscot and Passamaquoddy of Maine, sur-

vived in their original homelands. This was because white settlers in the more northern areas put less pressure on Natives to move. Groups farther south, such as the Powhatan, Nanticoke, Delaware, Pequot, and Abenaki, bore the full brunt of white settler pressure.

POWHATAN AND THE ENGLISH

Wahunsonacock, the leader of the Powhatan Confederacy (referred to simply as Powhatan by the English), did everything he could to help the English during their first difficult years at Jamestown. Despite this generosity, John Smith, the leader of the Jamestown colony, took an aggressive stand toward the Native Americans in the area, demanding them to submit to English rule and pay tribute (taxes) in the form of crops. Powhatan eventually became disillusioned with the English. He asked, "Why will you destroy us who supply you with food? What can you get by war?" He could not understand the English animosity toward the Indians nor could he understand their extreme desire for material gain. He did not want to go to war with them.

In 1609 John Smith was captured by members of the Powhatan Confedera-cy who suspected him of raiding one of their villages. Legend has it that Pocahontas, Powhatan's young daughter, interceded for Smith and saved him from execution. He was released and returned to Jamestown, but his policy toward Indians did not soften. Later, Pocahontas was captured by English settlers and eventually she converted to Christianity. In 1614 she married John Rolfe, the Englishman credited with beginning the European tobacco industry. She traveled to England, but soon died of an illness. In Virginia, the tobacco industry started by her husband required more and more Indian land, further aggravating relations between colonists and Indians. Although he had suffered personally and as the leader of his tribe, Powhatan continued to struggle for peace.

They had great difficulty in keeping their lands and traditions.

Great Lakes Groups

In the end, the peoples of the Great Lakes did not fare much better than coastal peoples. The Great Lakes region was inhabited by Shawnee, Fox, Sauk, Kickapoo, Winnebago, Menominee, Potawatomi, Chippewa, Ottawa, and other farming and hunting groups.

With a few exceptions, Great Lakes Natives did not come in contact with French traders until the late 1600s. Native people here, already aware of what had happened on the east coast, made efforts to slow the spread of European control. In 1763, Pontiac (an Ottawa chief) and, from 1805 to 1812, Tecumseh (a Shawnee warrior) brought tribal groups together to fight off the Europeans. But these rebellions were not successful in

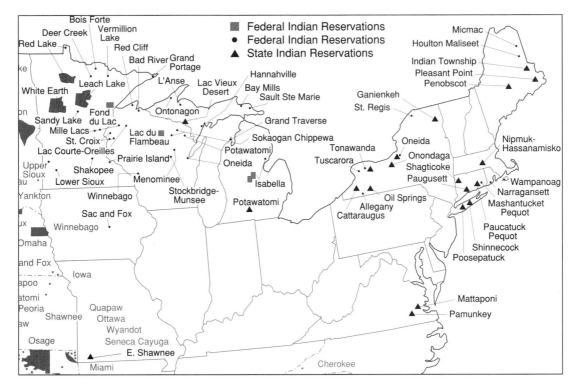

Contemporary Tribes of the northeastern United States.

the long run. By the late 1790s the once-powerful Iroquois nations had been relocated to reservations. By the 1860s most Native peoples of the Great Lakes regions had been assigned to small reservations. Other groups, such as the Shawnee and Delaware, were sent to reservations in Oklahoma.

For many years, Native American groups actively participated in the fur trade with Europeans. The fur trade greatly altered the methods of survival among the groups. After the decline of the fur trade, many Indians were no longer able to trade for the manufactured goods that had become central to their economic structures during the 1700s and 1800s. Without any alternative means

of support, some groups sold their lands and went to live on small reservations where the government promised them some support and protection.

Some tribes, such as the Ojibway (Chippewa), signed treaties that allowed them to keep their right to hunt and fish in their usual places. These treaty rights would become major issues in the 1970s and 1980s.

Iroquoian Peoples

Iroquoian is a word used to describe five New York nations—the Mohawk, Seneca, Cayuga, Onondaga, and Oneida—and other groups who spoke a language similar to the

Anishinabe man and woman gather wild rice from canoe in Minnesota.

Iroquoians'—such as the Huron, the Erie, and the Susquehannock. The early Iroquoian peoples shared a similar way of life, usually based on intensive farming, fishing, and hunting. Their villages were often palisaded (protected by barriers) because of a history of warfare with other Iroquois tribes and Algonkian people. Iroquoians lived in fairly large communities known for their **longhouses,** which were very long buildings that served as homes, places of worship, and places for community gatherings. Iroquoian societies were organized by **matrilineal** clans—groups of relatives who were related through the mother's side of the family.

In order to cement a trade alliance, French trader Samuel de Champlain joined a Huron and Algonquin raid on the Iroquois in 1609.

When Europeans arrived in their territories in the early 1500s, Iroquoian peoples lived along the St. Lawrence River in upper New York state, along the lower Great Lakes, and in the Susquehanna River Valley (in present-day Pennsylvania). We know more about these peoples than those who lived on the New England coast because European contact occurred more slowly in the area, allowing records to be made before disease, warfare, and trade had vastly changed the people and their culture.

Origin of the Iroquois Confederacy

The Five Nations of the Haudenosaunee, which means "People of the Longhouse," consisted of the Mohawk, Oneida, Ononda-ga, Cayuga, and Seneca. These nations formed a confederation (or association) some time between A.D. 1000 and 1350. From that time on, the Five Nations was governed by chiefs from the 49 families who were present at the origin of the confederacy.

The story of how the Iroquois confederacy began starts with Deganawidah, the Peacemaker, and his spokesperson, Hiawatha. Blood feuds had been dividing the Haudenosaunee people for years, and Deganawidah and Hiawatha wanted to stop the conflict. They planted a Great Tree of Peace at the Onondaga Nation, near present-day Syracuse, New York. Along with this symbolic tree planting, Deganawidah also passed down the Great Law, which is the constitution of the Iroquois confederacy. Deganawidah's Great Law instituted peace, unity, and clear thinking among the Haudenosaunee people.

The Strength of the Iroquois League

During the colonial period, the Iroquois confederacy's ability to unite with each other enabled them to present a strong front to ward off invaders. One of the reasons the Iroquois kept control of their important and strategic area of the Northeast was because the confederacy took in members of other Iroquoian groups, such as the Huron and Tuscarora, and therefore built up strength. Between 1650 and 1777, the Iroquois confederacy was at its most powerful. It stretched over a large area bounded by southeastern Ontario, New England, northern Pennsylvania, and northeastern Ohio. The Five Nations established a prosperous trade network by forming a trade alliance with the Dutch. In 1649 the Five Nations, armed with Dutch guns, initiated a series of wars with other Great Lakes tribes that traded with the French.

Iroquois Leaders Influence the New U.S. Government

With their long experience of confederation among tribes and trade relations with Europeans, the Iroquoian nations were very able politicians. They related to Europeans in various ways—through tact and diplomacy, neutrality, and finally by fortifying their inter-tribal alliance for increased strength. When the English began to move into their area, the Iroquois centralized their Confederate Council, which, as directed by their Great Law, was made up of 49 chiefs of the Five Nations. They allowed one chief to speak for the group.

In the 1700s, the newly forming U.S. government was aware of the great political skills of the Iroquoian nations. The founders of the new union wished to use the Five Nations as a model to create a confederacy of states based on unity, democracy, and liberty. Even before the Revolutionary War the Iroquois had counseled American leaders on the advantages of their style of confederation. The Iroquois influenced the Albany Plan of Union, written in 1755 to unite the colonies. They also greatly influenced the writing of the United States Constitution, the blueprint for the organization of the states into one united country.

The founding fathers invited Iroquois chiefs to attend the debates on the Declaration of Independence in Philadelphia in 1776. Over a period of weeks, the Iroquois watched the new nation emerge. They even gave the president of the group, John Hancock, an Iroquois name—"Karanduawn," which means "the Great Tree," the symbol of the birth of the Iroquois confederacy.

Other founders of the United States, such as Thomas Jefferson and John Adams, believed that the new U.S. government should be very similar to that of the Iroquois. In 1787 Jefferson stated that the "only condition on earth to be compared to [our government] is that of the Indians." John Adams asked the delegates at the Constitutional Convention to look to the Iroquois as a model. In 1790, Thomas Jefferson called the U.S. Constitution an Iroquois "tree of peace," recalling, again, the Iroquois symbol. He said this tree of peace would shelter Americans "with its branches of union."

Even though the founding fathers respected the Iroquois for their wisdom in

On June 11, 1776, an Onondoga sachem gave John Hancock an Iroquois name at Independence Hall. Drawing by John Kahiohes Fadden.

organizing governments, they did little to protect the Iroquois nations. Between 1777 and 1800, the government allowed various land companies to buy virtually all Iroquois lands. By 1880, the Iroquois had either left to live in Canada or were relocated to small reservations in upstate New York.

~quois Nations in the 20th Century

The Iroquois have survived as a nation nd they have struggled to maintain their ancient traditions. The Iroquois culture has had to change in order to support itself in modern America. Today, the Iroquois work in many professions of the American economy around them. They are ironworkers, steel workers, teachers, business people, and artists. But Iroquois languages are still spoken and taught. At the Onondoga Reservation, the Great Law set forth by Deganawidah is still recited. The Longhouse religion started by the Seneca prophet Handsome

String and belt wampum, c. 1890.

Lake in the 1830s has been revived. [Also see Religion chapter.]

Handsome Lake and his followers also revived the traditional chief system of leadership, and today it is present on the Onondaga, Tuscarora, and Tonawanda Seneca reservations in New York. In the Iroquoian chieftainship system, clan mothers nominate the chiefs of their clans. Chiefs are initiated to office through an ancient condolence ceremony. Great festivals with traditional readings and thanksgiving ceremonies are attended by many Iroquois from both cities and reservations.

Treaty Rights

On a number of fronts, modern Iroquois people are insisting on the rights they were given by treaty. They have filed claims against the U.S. government for the loss of their lands and other treaty rights. They have also fought for the return of sacred artifacts, which are often held by museums, universities, and the government. After a generation of struggle, historic Iroquois **wampum belts** that had been held at the New York State Museum were returned. Wampum belts are ceremonial records made from polished shells on a string or chain of several rows. Symbols were embroidered into the belts as historical records of agreements, treaties, important events, and sacred law. The Iroquois wanted the belts returned so they can be used by those who appreciate

44

Members of the Iroquois League protesting for their rights to cross U.S.-Canadian border in accordance with the Jay Treaty.

and understand their value. The Iroquois continue to use wampum belts as a record of important events.

The Iroquois are active in international forums on native rights. Since the early 1900s, the Iroquois Confederacy has issued its own passports. These passports are recognized for travel purposes by many nations, thereby showing that they recognize the sovereignty of the Iroquois nation.

Since the 1920s, the Iroquois have staged "border crossings" into Canada each summer. They stage these crossings to assert the right given them by Jay's Treaty in 1794, to move freely across the U.S.-Canada border. In these and other ways, the Iroquois strive to keep their culture alive and to exercise their independence as a nation. [Also see Canada's Native Peoples and Their Lands chapter.]

4

Native Groups of the Southeast

Major Culture Areas

FACT FOCUS

- The Green Corn Ceremony, usually held in mid-summer among Southeastern cultures, has been compared to a combination of Thanksgiving, New Year's, Yom Kippur, and Mardi Gras.
- The Cherokee called women of great influence "Beloved Women." They called women who fought in wars "War Women."
- The Cherokee developed a writing system and, from 1828 to 1835, published a weekly newspaper written in both Cherokee and English.
- An estimated four thousand Cherokee died on the Trail of Tears, the enforced march to Oklahoma.
- Women have a powerful role in Cherokee society today. This is reflected in the election of Wilma Mankiller as tribal chair of the Western Cherokee in 1987 and 1991.
- Many Southeastern Native American groups played a ball game similar to lacrosse.

[See Chapter 3: Native Groups of the Northeast for an introduction to the study of major culture areas.]

Southeast Culture before European Contact

When Europeans reached the southeastern United States they found many Native peoples who were emerging from the Mississippian culture, which came into being in around A.D. 800. The southeastern villagers built ceremonial mounds in their town centers and cultivated fields of corn, beans, and squash. Although these earthen mounds were no longer used very much by the 1500s, the lives of the Native people were still centered around village life and farming. The Catawba, Cherokee, Creek, Chickasaw, Choctaw, and Seminole descended from these peoples.

The Southeast (shaded).

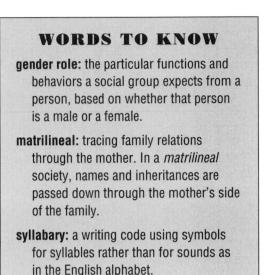

WORDS TO KNOW

gender role: the particular functions and behaviors a social group expects from a person, based on whether that person is a male or a female.

matrilineal: tracing family relations through the mother. In a *matrilineal* society, names and inheritances are passed down through the mother's side of the family.

syllabary: a writing code using symbols for syllables rather than for sounds as in the English alphabet.

Most villages of Southeastern peoples were run by a council of elders and warriors, headed by a chief. The chief usually came to power because of special talents or skills, or by belonging to an important family or clan. In most of these societies, families were organized by the mother's line of relatives. Clan membership was an extremely important aspect of these societies.

Southeastern tribes were made up of loosely organized groups of villages. They had similar languages and customs, and lived close to one another. Leaders of the villages were given only limited power— usually they were only as powerful as their skills in persuading people to go along with their ideas. Even if a village voted to sup-

port a war or a treaty, the members could withdraw their support at any time if they changed their minds. At that point they would become free from any further obligation. The Southeastern groups placed high value on personal freedom and social harmony. This was a constant source of frustration to Europeans who wanted to have fixed, permanent rules and treaties.

Achieving balance and harmony among human beings, nature, and the spirit world was a central religious belief held by Southeastern peoples. All things had spirits, either good or evil, and all success in life depended on treating these spirits with respect and honor, it was held. An act of disharmony— even a serious act like murder—could be fixed by the proper remedy.

The Southeastern Green Corn Ceremony was an elaborate thanksgiving and renewal festival, usually held in mid-summer. The success of the corn crop was very important it promised food for winter and seeds for the

Oseola, a Seminole. Artwork by George Catlin.

less killing might anger the spirits of the game. [Also see Religion chapter.]

Southeastern peoples also shared an interest in games, especially a ball game played by teams from competing villages on a level field about two hundred yards long. In this game a deerskin ball stuffed with deer or squirrel hair was used. In some versions the players carried two sticks to scoop up the ball and forward it. The object was to throw the ball past the opposition's goal post at the other end of the field.

Two rituals common among Southeastern cultures were the use of the black drink and sacred tobacco. The black drink, as the Europeans called it, was a tea made from the roasted leaves of the yaupon holly. Like coffee, it contained caffeine and left people highly stimulated. It was often used before a major celebration or decision. The sacred (or "white") tobacco was used in diplomatic ceremonies and to welcome visitors. It was put in a pipe and passed around the circle for all to share.

European Contact

When Europeans arrived, the harmony and balance in the lives of Southeastern peoples was shattered. The first recorded visit by Europeans was led by Spanish adventurer Hernando de Soto in 1540 and 1541. De Soto and other explorers brought diseases for which the Natives had no immunity (natural defenses). Native Americans died by the thousands. De Soto's army was particularly ruthless in its treatment of Native peoples, slaughtering Indian warriors and kidnapping women as it traveled through the area. French and English explorers soon arrived,

next spring. If a crop failed, starvation and death might follow. "We would have something approaching the Green Corn Ceremony," American anthropologist Charles Hudson once said, "if we combined Thanksgiving, New Year's festivities, Yom Kippur, and Mardi Gras."

In addition to farming, Southeastern peoples also hunted. Like farming, hunting was connected to the spirit world. Hunters prayed to the spirits of the game before hunting. They believed that if they didn't, the animal spirits might be offended and refuse to allow game to be killed the next time. And, the hunter killed no more than he needed—use-

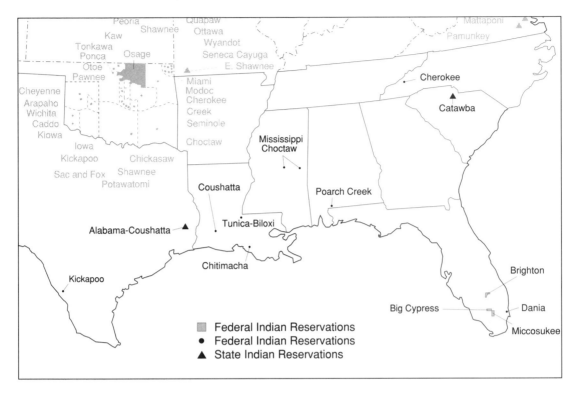

Contemporary southeastern tribes.

The map shows the following tribes and reservations:

Peoria, Shawnee, Quapaw, Ottawa, Wyandot, Seneca Cayuga, E. Shawnee, Kaw, Tonkawa, Ponca, Osage, Otoe, Pawnee, Cheyenne, Arapaho, Wichita, Caddo, Kiowa, Miami, Modoc, Cherokee, Creek, Seminole, Choctaw, Iowa, Kickapoo, Sac and Fox, Shawnee, Potawatomi, Chickasaw, Coushatta, Alabama-Coushatta, Kickapoo, Tunica-Biloxi, Chitimacha, Mississippi Choctaw, Poarch Creek, Cherokee, Catawba, Mattaponi, Pamunkey, Brighton, Big Cypress, Dania, Miccosukee

■ Federal Indian Reservations
● Federal Indian Reservations
▲ State Indian Reservations

competing with the Spanish for new lands and domination of the people on them.

The Impact of Trade

The European trade in skins and furs changed the lives of Native peoples forever. Before trade was established, deer were hunted only as needed and care was taken to maintain the herds. But the fur trade demanded more and more skins, and the deer population had declined by the 1730s.

Because resources were used to purchase goods from European traders, many Southeastern groups quit, or drastically reduced, the production of their traditional crafts. Handmade clothing, tools, decorative ob-

jects, and other items began to disappear. Manufactured goods from Europe were attractive to the villagers, especially novelty items such as mirrors, knives, scissors, and jews harps. Alcohol, another new commodity introduced by European traders, greatly changed Native American social patterns.

Gender roles also changed. Gender roles are the ways in which men and women in a particular society are expected to act because of their sex. Southeastern societies were **matrilineal,** meaning that heredity was traced through the mother's side of the family. Women in most southeastern cultures had long been respected and valued as child-bearers, food-providers, and craftspeople.

Indians in North Carolina fishing with traps, spears, and nets. Artwork by John White, 1885.

When trading with Europeans became a major source of income within a village, however, the roles of women began to be seen as less important. Hunting was the most important activity because it brought trade goods. The traditional handicrafts that women had practiced for thousands of years quickly lost their value, and many women stopped producing them.

When traders began to live in the Native villages, their households were usually male dominated, as in the European tradition. When traders married Native women, their children generally grew up following European ways. As the number of mixed marriages increased, the number of homes that were run in the traditional Southeastern way decreased greatly. By the end of the 1700s,

many villages were controlled by mixed trader families. In many cases, mixed-blood leaders were more willing to sign treaties and sell Native homelands than full-blooded Natives might have been.

The Cherokee

The Cherokee Indians once lived in the southern Appalachian mountains. Today they live in a variety of areas. The Eastern Band lives in western North Carolina, on or near the Qualla Boundary (the name of their reservation). The Western Band lives in Oklahoma. Many people from both groups live and work throughout the United States. Those who keep their language alive speak an Iroquoian language.

In the late 1600s, there were about 30,000 Cherokee living in about 60 villages. One hundred years later, there were only 7,500 Cherokee people left alive. The Cherokee had been killed off by smallpox and other epidemic diseases, warfare, and enforced removal in harsh conditions from their homelands. Today, however, there are more than 175,000 Western Cherokee and more than 9,500 Eastern Cherokee.

Europeans first visited the Cherokee in the southern Appalachians in the 1600s. Cherokee villages were located in mountain river valleys where there was space for houses, council houses, and farm fields.

The Cherokee were a matrilineal society. Their fields were controlled by the Cherokee women. Women who had great influence or power became known as Beloved Women. Beloved Women often worked behind the scenes to help shape major decisions. A woman could take her husband's place in war, in which case she was given the title War Woman. Women still have a powerful role in Cherokee society today. This is reflected in the election of Wilma Mankiller as tribal chair of the Western Cherokee in 1987 and 1991.

Fighting to Keep Homelands

From 1783 to 1835 the Cherokee fought a powerful and primarily nonviolent battle to keep their lands from white settlers. By 1825 some had already moved to Texas and Arkansas in hopes of escaping the Americans. But many tried to fight the system they had seen taking land away from other Native groups.

In 1823 Sequoyah, a Cherokee living in present-day Arkansas, had developed a system of writing using a **syllabary**—a writing code using symbols for syllables rather than for sounds as in the English alphabet. [Also see Language chapter.] Many Cherokee quickly learned to read and write in the Cherokee syllabary. From 1828 to 1835 the *Cherokee Phoenix,* a weekly newspaper printed in both English and Cherokee, was published and widely read.

In the early 1820s the Cherokee established a capital in New Echota, Georgia. They wrote a constitution for a government in 1827 that was, in many ways, similar to the U.S. Constitution. They wished to establish their own government and the right to preserve their homelands in Georgia, Tennessee, and Alabama. The Georgia legislature, however, wanting to remove the Cherokee from the territory, passed a series of laws that abolished the Cherokee government and appropriated (took for itself) Cherokee land.

When the state of Georgia tried to remove the Cherokee from their homeland, the Cherokee took the case to the Supreme Court. They based their case on a clause in the Constitution that allows foreign nations to seek redress (compensation or remedy) in the Supreme Court for damages caused by U.S. citizens. The court ruled that Indian nations are not foreign nations, but dependent, domestic nations. Up until that time, U.S. law had treated Indian nations as separate, or foreign, nations. Although the Cherokee lost this case, in a case in 1832 the Supreme Court ruled that Georgia could not remove the Cherokee from their land, stating that only the federal government had the right to regulate Indian affairs; states could not extend their laws over Indian governments. But this victory won by the Cherokee was temporary.

The Trail of Tears

In 1835, a small group of tribal leaders (who were mainly of mixed blood) signed the Treaty of New Echota. This treaty caused Cherokee living in South Carolina, Georgia, Tennessee, and Alabama to be evicted from their homelands. Even though 15,000 Cherokee signed a petition against the treaty, the government still forced them out. The U.S. government imprisoned any Cherokee who refused to abandon their lands, and burned their homes and crops.

In the late fall and winter of 1838 and 1839, between 13,000 and 16,000 Cherokee were marched by Andrew Jackson and his army on the "Trail of Tears" on foot to Oklahoma. Between 25 and 35 percent of the Cherokee died during this march, an estimated 4,000 to 8,000 people. Other Southeastern tribes forced to walk to Oklahoma in

Cherokee boy and girl in costume on reservation, North Carolina.

similar marches, including the Choctaw, Chickasaw, Creek and Seminole, suffered similar losses. One of Jackson's soldiers wrote: "I fought through the Civil War and have seen men shot to pieces and slaughtered by thousands, but the Cherokee removal was the cruelest work I ever knew."

In North Carolina about 1,000 Cherokee escaped removal with the help of state officials who were sympathetic to them. One North Carolinian, William H. Thomas (called Wil-Usdi by the Cherokee), bought land in his name for the Cherokee, went to court in

their defense, and even visited Washington on their behalf.

The Western Cherokee

When the majority of the Cherokee arrived in Indian Territory (present-day Oklahoma) they tried to establish a workable government, avoid disputes with rival tribes, and maintain relations with the federal government. But even in the west, the Cherokee were not allowed to keep their lands. One way or another—through bribery, threats, or manipulation—the Cherokee lands were sold to non-Natives. By 1907 almost all of their fertile or mineral-rich lands were owned by non-Cherokee. [Also see Oklahoma chapter.]

But today the Western Cherokee are growing in numbers and in power. Led by Principal Chief Wilma Mankiller, the Cherokee have sought to rebuild their communities. Both small and large community projects have given the Cherokee a renewed spirit. For example, men, women, and children laid 16 miles of pipe for running water in the tiny village of Bell. They also built a hydroelectric plant worth millions of dollars. Farming operations and defense plants have been started. Wilma Mankiller says that the key to their success is that Cherokee never give up!

The Eastern Cherokee

After World War II, some economic recovery came to the Eastern Cherokee in western North Carolina in the form of highways, a national park, and the tourist industry. The roads were developed for access to the Great Smoky Mountains National Park, next to the Cherokee homeland. By the early 1950s, the Cherokee Historical Association produced "Unto These Hills," a drama based on the Cherokee experience. It attracts many visitors, as do the Oconoluftee Village and the Museum of the Cherokee Indian. All aim to give tourists a realistic look at Cherokee life and culture.

These developments have resulted in good incomes for only a few Cherokee, however. Many still live in poverty. One potential income-producer is the building of an enormous bingo parlor, where almost four thousand people can play for prizes worth thousands of dollars.

In an attempt to provide jobs for their children, the Eastern Cherokee bought the Carolina Mirror Company in 1986 at a cost of $28.8 million. Jobs will allow the Cherokee to support themselves in a non-Indian economy, while maintaining their self-reliance.

5

Native Groups of the Southwest

Major Culture Areas

FACT FOCUS

- During a drought in the 1930s, the U.S. government killed tens of thousands of Navajo sheep, saying that the animals' grazing had eroded the land and created the "dust bowl."
- The Hopi never signed a treaty with the United States because the two nations never entered into open fighting.
- When the United States annexed New Mexico in 1848, the Pueblo, who had full Mexican citizenship, automatically became U.S. citizens.

[See Chapter 3: Native Groups of the Northeast for an introduction to the study of major culture areas.]

Early Southwest Culture

Before European colonization, the area that is now the southwestern United States and northern Mexico was called Aztlán. Aztlán was named by the Aztecs, who built a powerful empire in central Mexico. After the Mexican-American War, from 1846 to 1848, the northern part of Aztlán became the southwestern United States.

Many agricultural (farming) communities developed in Aztlán. By about A.D. 900,

these consisted of multistory villages (later named **pueblos**) and large ceremonial centers. The ceremonial centers resembled kivas, the round underground chambers found among the present-day Hopi in Arizona and the Pueblo in eastern New Mexico.

Between A.D. 900 and 1200, major trade centers and ceremonial towns emerged at Canyon de Chelly and Chaco Canyon. About one to two hundred towns existed here, connected by walkways. People of these communities traded amongst each other and with distant cities as far away as Central America and the Pacific Coast.

An extreme drought between 1275 and 1300 caused the southwestern peoples to

The Southwest (shaded).

leave their towns and move closer to fresh water sources. The Hopi moved to the Colorado River area, while most others moved to present-day New Mexico along the Rio Grande River. By 1540, when the Spanish began to explore northern Mexico, the population in the Southwest was about two hundred thousand people.

The Navajo and Apache also lived in the Southwest. They were hunters and gatherers and lived in small bands that spread over a seven-hundred-square-mile territory, including all of present-day New Mexico and Arizona. They traded and intermarried with the more settled village peoples and became involved in their wars.

Because of their close contact with the Pueblo, the Navajo and Apache adopted important aspects of Pueblo culture. For example, the Navajo combined some parts of Pueblo creation stories with their own. Some Apache groups adopted Pueblo ceremonies—in particular the **Kachina** dance costumes. (In Pueblo traditions, the Kachina were benevolent ancestral spirit beings.)

Spanish Colonization

When the Spanish began to colonize in the early 1600s, they forcefully controlled the village peoples, forbidding them to practice

At Mesa Verde, Colorado, multistoried pueblos were built to take advantage of the shelter offered by rock overhangs.

their ceremonies and rituals. Many Pueblos were forced to work on the ranches and farms of the Spanish officers and upper class.

By 1628, Spanish **missionaries** had demanded that native people **convert** to Christianity and abandon their traditional religions. Young Pueblos were forced into the Spanish army, whose main function was to make slave raids into nearby areas. For 200 years, the Navajo, Apache, and Ute (a hunting and gathering people who lived in what is now Colorado) defended themselves ferociously against these slave raids.

In 1680 the Pueblo spiritual leader, Pope, led his people in a rebellion that forced the Spanish and their Indian allies to move to present-day El Paso, Texas. But Spanish military forces regained control, and by 1696 many Pueblos had left their villages to join the Navajo bands to the north. Navajo bands began to raid Spanish farms and the Pueblos for horses, cattle, sheep, and manufactured goods. Eventually, during the 1700s many Navajo began to herd sheep, which some continue to do today.

During the early 1700s, the Comanche migrated to New Mexico from present-day Wyoming. By the mid-1700s, the Comanche had gained control of the horse and gun trade on the southern Plains. They had become the

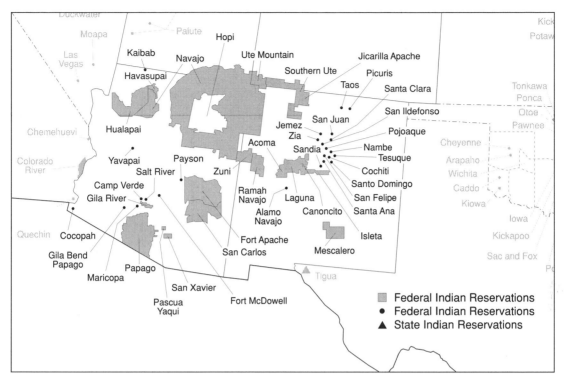

Contemporary southwestern tribes.

most powerful bison-hunting tribe in the area.

From the late 1700s to the mid-1800s, much warfare and raiding took place among the Spanish, Pueblos, and Apache and Navajo. The U.S. Army and traders entered the Southwest in full force after the Mexican-American War in 1848. There they met strong resistance from Indian peoples.

The Navajo Nation

The Navajo Nation is the largest Native nation in the United States. The Navajo reservation, located in Arizona and New Mexico, covers 17 million acres—about the size of the state of West Virginia. There are about 175,000 Navajo, and their population may reach as many as 250,000 people by the year 2000.

In the mid-1800s, the U.S. military tried to subdue the Indians in the Southwest and control their land. Many Navajo cornfields were burned, fruit trees were destroyed, sheep were slaughtered, and communities were ruined. The Navajo successfully resisted for 17 years. But, facing starvation in 1863 and 1864, they finally surrendered.

Christopher (Kit) Carson, a New Mexico trader, was made a colonel in the U.S. Army. During the 1860s he led an army of volunteers to capture and settle first the Apache and then numerous Navajo bands. Over 8,000 Navajo were rounded up and driven to

Navajo women sheering sheep.

Bosque Redondo, a camp in eastern New Mexico far from their homeland. The Navajo called the reservation Hweedli (prison). There, more than 2,000 Navajo died from starvation and exposure (lack of shelter). In 1868 a treaty was made with the Navajo and they were allowed to settle on the present-day Navajo reservation.

After the Navajo settled on the reservation, the U.S. government ignored them until 1922, when oil was discovered on their lands. Previously these lands had been considered useless. When oil was found, the government created the Navajo Business Council to grant oil and mineral leases in the name of the Navajo nation.

The Navajo firmly rejected the Indian Reorganization Act of 1934, which would have given them a federally structured tribal government and constitution. Instead, they held their own constitutional convention, with the federal government's permission. The Navajo wrote a constitution which would give them independence from the Bureau of Indian Affairs (BIA).

The U.S. government rejected this plan, and instead formed a new Navajo Business Council. This council was composed of 74 elected Navajo members and became known as the "Rules of 1938." It was the basis for the present Navajo Tribal Council.

During the late 1930s an extreme drought

A Navajo woman stands next to her traditional hogan in Tuba City, Arizona.

made the central and southern United States so dry the affected area was called the "dust bowl." At this time, the U.S. government decided that the Navajo were raising too many sheep and that the grazing would cause land erosion. Agents of the Agricultural Department killed tens of thousands of Navajo sheep. For several decades after this, relations between the Navajo and the U.S. government were hostile.

The Navajo Reservation Economy Today

At present, most of the Navajo lands are used for grazing sheep, cattle, and goats. Although the Navajo grow grain to feed their livestock, they own almost five million acres of additional land that could be used for farming. However, the main income generated by the land is from development of natural resources, such as oil, gas, coal, and uranium in which the territory is rich. Five hundred thousand acres of commercial forest on Navajo lands yield millions of dollars of income each year.

There is still a wide gap between the wealth of the Navajo lands and the welfare of the Navajo people, who are mostly poor. Navajo per capita income (the amount of money earned for each person) is only $1,000 per year. Unemployment is about 50

The Navajo Nation officially welcomed home all Navajo service men and women who served in the Persian Gulf War in 1991. Approximately 450 Navajo served in the Gulf.

percent. Many of the unemployed are unskilled and lack formal education, and many speak little English. Services such as day-care centers are lacking. About 75 percent of employed Navajo work in jobs funded by the U.S. government. The rest work in other occupations, such as commercial farming, mining, forestry, and trade.

The Navajo Form Unions

In the 1970s, the Navajo began to work in industry. There they found racial discrimination in pay and in duties assigned. As a result, the Navajo formed trade unions, which had been banned on the reservation. By the late 1970s, almost all Navajo workers working for private firms (rather than for the government) were members of labor unions. The higher wages resulting from unionized jobs, combined with traditional Native practices of sharing and generosity among family and clan, have helped to raise the standard of living among the Navajo.

About 20 percent of Navajo people live off the reservation. Many of these relocated to California. For economic and other reasons, migration to and from the reservation is constant.

Navajo People Move toward Self-Determination

The Navajo have actively pursued the goal of self-determination in their communities. Navajo Community College, the first tribal college in the United States, was established on the Navajo reservation in 1971. The college was so successful that over two dozen other tribal colleges have been founded, and many more are planned. [Also see Education chapter.]

In 1959 the Navajo adopted a court system modeled after the U.S. legal system. The Navajo did not want the states of New Mexico and Arizona to extend their court systems onto the reservation, so they established their own courts, applying their own ideas of justice. The Navajo often settle problems in a traditional manner, rather than by following U.S. law. For example, they try to bring opposing parties together to solve their problems, rather than trying cases to decide who is at fault and issuing penalties. [Also see Law, Treaties, and Land Claims chapter.]

Before the 1950s, the Navajo government was not well supported by its people, who preferred to form local groups with their own leaders. In response, the Navajo government has made efforts to include representatives from local areas. Based on traditional ideas and customs, the Navajo tribal government is the largest organization of its kind in North America.

The Hopi

The Hopi are descended from the earliest inhabitants of the Southwest. They have occupied a large part of present-day northern Arizona for centuries. At present their reservation is entirely surrounded by the large Navajo reservation.

The Hopi are a farming people, raising several types of corn, beans, squash, and other plants. Traditionally, men hunted animals such as deer and elk, and the women gathered nuts, fruits, and roots.

Hopi society is divided into twelve groups of clans called "phratries." Children always belong to the clan of their mother. Clans are very important for social and religious purposes, and each clan has its own special sacred objects and ceremonies.

Each Hopi clan shares a version of the same creation story in which their ancestors originally came to earth from a world below to seek peace and balance. The Hopi believe they must honor the spirits in order to be successful. Many Hopi (as well as Pueblo) ceremonies aim to create harmony in the community and to please the Kachina spirits so they will bring rain to the dry land for Hopi crops.

In the middle and late 1500s, there may have been as many as a dozen Hopi villages along the Colorado River. The populations of these villages dropped severely because many people died of the diseases brought by Spanish explorers. By 1600 most Hopi had retreated to their present villages in northern Arizona. There the Spanish tried to rule the Hopi and spread Christianity, but the Hopi resisted.

Walpi, an ancient Hopi Pueblo village.

Because the Hopi never entered into open fighting with the United States, no treaty was ever signed to give them legal title to their homelands. The Navajo, whose lands encircle the Hopi lands, entered into a treaty with the United States for their lands in northwestern New Mexico and northeastern Arizona. In 1882 the Hopi complained that Navajo families were settling on their lands. The Hopi reservation was then established by executive order, but Hopi lands continued to be settled by Navajo and Mormon settlers.

After growing conflict between the Hopi and the Navajo, U.S. courts created a Joint Use Area—1.8 million acres to be shared by the two nations. Only a portion of the Hopi reservation was reserved for the exclusive use of the Hopi. In 1973 clashes broke out between the Hopi and the Navajo over the Joint Use Area. In 1974 Congress passed the Hopi and Navajo Relocation Act. The Joint Use Area was divided between the two nations, and $16 million compensation was provided to eight hundred Navajo families who were required to relocate.

Hopi child clown.

Today the Hopi occupy about 12 villages on the Hopi reservation. Many live in pueblos in the traditional ways and resist U.S. cultural influences in religion, education, and government. But a long-standing division among the people began during the 1930s and continues today. The Hopi divided over whether to accept or reject the Indian Reorganization Act (IRA) of 1934. The IRA allowed reservation communities to vote to reorganize their governments along the U.S democratic model and to create tribal economic corporations. Although the IRA was meant to give Indian communities more control, many Hopi rejected it because it did not fit their traditional way of life. They wanted a Hopi government, based on traditional Hopi customs and religion.

Conservative Hopi (those who wish to save, or "conserve" traditional ways) are some of the most active nationalist groups in the United States. They have appealed to organizations such as the United Nations for justice over broken treaty agreements and for recognition of their independence. Other Hopi, however, were willing to live under an IRA government and to accept some parts of Western ways along with their traditional ways.

The Pueblo Villages of New Mexico

The Spanish arrived at the northern Rio Grande River in the 1500s. There they found 98 villages, which they called pueblos. A few decades later there were only 19 villages, all of which exist today.

Pueblo peoples have similar cultures, but they speak four distinct languages: Zuni, Keres, Tiwa, and Tewa. Many continue to speak their native languages; most speak English also. Each pueblo is self-governed and fiercely independent, but they all participate in the All Indian Pueblo Council, which is a loose federation (or grouping).

The All Indian Pueblo Council began with the Pueblo Revolt against the Spanish in 1680. Pope, a religious leader from San Juan Pueblo, led the successful drive to force the Spanish and some of their Pueblo allies out of Pueblo territory. With the Spanish gone, the Pueblo enjoyed freedom for about 12 years, but in 1695 the Spanish conquered the Pueblo once again. Many Pueblo did not want to live under Spanish rule, so they went to live among Navajo and Apache bands.

The Pueblo who remained under Spanish rule were forced to **convert** to Catholicism. Many were made to work on the ranches of Spanish officers and other wealthy people. From 1821 to 1848, the Pueblo were ruled by independent Mexico. They were the only Southwest Indians who had full Mexican citizenship. As Mexican citizens the Pueblo people automatically became U.S. citizens when the United States annexed the area in 1848.

As U.S. citizens, the Pueblo did not receive the rights and protection granted to Indians as independent nations by the federal government. As a result, much Pueblo land, which was the finest farmland in the Southwest, was lost.

The Pueblo asked for, and then sued for, Indian status, which they gained in 1916. Meanwhile, they had lost some of their best lands as well as important religious sites. The All Indian Pueblo Council organized delegates from all the pueblos in an effort to regain their land. The resulting Pueblo Lands Act of 1924 restored Pueblo lands, but the battle is not over. Today the Pueblo fight hard to get and keep their water rights. Their lands are secure, but useless without water.

An important victory for the Pueblo was won in 1975. At that time, the sacred area of Blue Lake and 55,000 surrounding acres of land were returned to the Taos Pueblo. They had struggled for 30 years for the return of this sacred land, which they consider the navel of the universe and the place where the Creator first created people. The people of Taos Pueblo hold annual ceremonies at Blue Lake, which they believe ensures their well-being and prosperity. The return of Blue Lake gave other Indian peoples hope that they might be successful in regaining and protecting their sacred areas.

During the 1960s and 1970s, Zuni Pueblo became known as the model of Indian peoples' efforts to recover management of their community from the government. The Zuni did not want the government to run their affairs, so in the late 1960s they gained control of community programs previously run by the Bureau of Indian Affairs (BIA). The Zuni ran many of their programs more effectively than the BIA had done, and more members of the community participated.

Christmas Day Matachine dancers at San Juan Pueblo.

The success of the Zuni came to the attention of President Richard Nixon and, in 1970, he announced the government's policy to support Indian self-determination. This granted tribal governments greater control over their community programs and schools. President Nixon held up the Zuni as an example to all Indian communities who wished to play a greater role in their local affairs.

The 19 New Mexico pueblos remain strongly traditional communities. There are many well-known artists, novelists, poets, scholars, and painters among the Pueblo, including Paula Gunn Allen, Alfonso Ortiz, and Leslie Marmon Silko.

6

Native Groups of the Northern Plains

Major Culture Areas

FACT FOCUS

- During the last half of the 1800s, non-Indian hunters slaughtered so many buffalo that the species nearly became extinct. Buffalo was the major food source of many Plains tribes.
- The Ghost Dance movement offered a vision of the end of the world, when dead ancestors would return, Europeans would disappear, and life on the North American continent would return to old Indian ways.
- On December 24, 1890, the U.S. Army opened fire on followers of the Ghost Dance movement, killing 370 men, women, and children at Wounded Knee.
- Until 1952, a law was in place that banned the sale of alcohol to Native Americans.

[See Chapter 3: Native Groups of the Northeast for an introduction to the study of major culture areas.]

Migration to the Plains

One of the most common images of Indian people in popular American culture is that of the Plains culture, with its fierce warriors, sacred **Sun Dance** ceremonies, horsemanship, and buffalo hunting. However, the Plains culture was a relatively short-lived way of life. It only lasted about two hundred years and was not typical of the way Native American cultures had lived for centuries before.

About eight to ten thousand years ago, all horses in North America died out. Much later, in the 1500s, wild horses (American mustangs) that had escaped from the early Spanish explorers came to live on the Plains. At that time only a few of the nations who would later make up the High Plains Culture were living on the Plains. They lived in small huts and hunted buffalo on foot. Most Indian nations now regarded as Plains tribes lived farther east.

The Northern Plains (shaded).

Most Plains Indians **migrated** onto the Plains after 1650, when European expansion and trade forced many Indians westward. The Iroquois in upstate New York pushed west to gain access to land with fur-bearing animals, which were necessary for trade with Europeans. The Iroquois expansion created a domino effect, as nations pushed each other farther west in their quest for fur. The impact was felt by distant cultures, as the following example shows.

By moving into their territory, the Iroquois pushed the Chippewa and Ottawa west into the upper Great Lakes area. During the 1700s and 1800s, the Chippewa moved into present-day Minnesota. Armed with guns from European traders, they began pushing the Sioux Indians from their woodland homes in Minnesota onto the Plains during the late 1700s. By the early 1800s, many Sioux bands had moved onto the Plains. There they became accomplished horse riders and buffalo hunters. They practiced the Sun Dance, a dance of sacrifice for the well-being of the community. They also began raiding the villages of farming peoples who lived along the Missouri River, such as the Mandan, Arikara, and Hidatsa.

Before they moved onto the Plains, the Cheyenne lived in present-day southern Canada. Pushed west by the Iroquois, the Cheyenne were living in present-day Min-

Assiniboine Indians hunting bison. Painting by Paul Kane from his travels in the 1840s.

nesota by the 1700s. By the late 1700s, they were living in eastern North Dakota. Originally farmers and hunters, in their new home they also began using horses and hunting buffalo, while growing corn crops.

The Plains Culture

By the mid-1800s, the Cheyenne had moved to the western plains and had fully adopted the Plains culture. They practiced the Sun Dance ceremony, had military societies of young men, and lived in portable teepees. In the summer they gathered to celebrate religious ceremonies; in the winter the Cheyenne (like other Plains nations such as the Sioux, Blackfeet, and Crow) broke up into small bands and spent the cold winter months in separate locations.

Often the **indigenous** Indian peoples (those who were there originally) considered the newcomers hostile intruders. The original Plains Indians, like the Pawnee and Ponca, tried to defend their traditional hunting territories. The newly arrived eastern Indians tried to recreate their communities in the Plains territory. It was no surprise that conflict resulted.

Destruction of the Plains Culture

Despite conflicts between groups, the Plains culture flourished during the 1700s and much of the 1800s. It ended when the U.S. government placed the Plains Indians on reservations. Starting in 1830, the U.S. gov-

Sioux Sun Dance. Artwork by Jules Tavernier and Paul Frenzeny, 1874.

ernment began to move most Indian nations east of the Mississippi to new homelands west of the Mississippi. Most were moved to present-day Kansas and Oklahoma.

By the 1880s, non-Indian hunters had slaughtered the large herds of buffalo; in fact, there were only about one thousand buffalo left at that time. Without adequate supplies of buffalo for food, the Indian Plains Culture could not survive. Often faced with the threat of starvation, Plains Indians had little choice but to move to the reservations.

The Battle of Little Bighorn

Around 1876, gold was discovered in the Black Hills of South Dakota, which is sacred land for the Sioux. As gold miners began their work, several groups of Sioux left the reservations to protect the Black Hills from **sacrilege.** Led by Crazy Horse of the Oglala Sioux and Sitting Bull of the Hunkpapa band of Teton Sioux, the Indians gathered to face the U.S. Army, which was protecting the gold miners. Colonel George Armstrong Custer and his Seventh Cavalry were sent to Little Bighorn Valley (in present-day Montana) to head off the Sioux. The Sioux and Cheyenne, however, met Custer's advance and killed all of the 225-man troop, including Custer himself.

The Lakota (the name the Sioux have for themselves), Cheyenne, and Blackfeet con-

"Trail of the hide hunters." Buffalo lying dead in snow, 1872.

tinued to fight battles with the United States, trying to keep settlers and miners from staying in the area. Two of these battles were the Sand Creek Battle of 1864 and the Bozeman Trail War (1866-68).

By 1880, reservation life was the only option for Plains Indians, and many reluctantly moved. The Cheyenne, for example, resisted removal to Oklahoma in the 1870s, but eventually they settled onto the Tongue River reservation in eastern Montana. In 1916 a group of Plains Chippewa and Cree found refuge on the Rocky Boy Reservation in Montana. Eventually, most Plains Indians settled on reservations. People often gathered to live near relatives, and these groupings eventually became the present-day reservation communities.

The Ghost Dance Movement and Wounded Knee

After their buffalo culture had been destroyed and the people had been placed

Bird's eye view of Sioux camp at Pine Ridge, South Dakota, 1890.

on reservations, the Plains Indians found solace and hope in the Ghost Dance revitalization movement. The Ghost Dance ceremony expressed a vision of the end of the present world, in which all the dead Indian ancestors and the near-extinct game animals would return. The end of the present world meant that the continent would return to its state before Europeans had arrived there.

In 1889 many Sioux were dying of starvation due to a drought. Although Congress promised food rations, they were delayed in arriving while people went hungry. Epidemics ravaged the reservations. The Sioux began to see the Ghost Dance movement as a means of spiritual resistance to U.S. authority. [Also see Religion chapter.]

Government agents and local settlers, however, feared an Indian uprising like the one at Little Bighorn, and they set out to suppress the new religion, outlawing it in 1890. When Sioux leader Sitting Bull was killed by Indian police, other followers of the Ghost Dance movement fled south to Pine Ridge Reservation. Just a few miles from Pine Ridge, at Wounded Knee Creek, on December 24, 1890, Custer's old regiment, the Seventh Cavalry, opened fire on the Indians with machine guns. They mowed down everything alive—warriors, old people, women, children, ponies, and dogs. Three

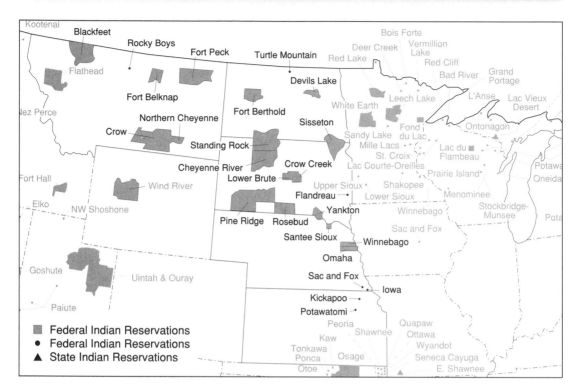

Contemporary Plains Indians tribes.

hundred seventy Indians were massacred; 250 of them were women and children.

Maintaining the Plains Culture

Despite U.S. attempts to end the **tribalism**—loyalty to the group—that was so strong among the Northern Plains Indians, the contemporary Plains tribes have fought hard to preserve their cultural life and heritage.

After 1880, schools and mission churches were often built near reservation villages in an attempt to introduce the "American" way of life. Many Plains Indians resisted by keeping their children home.

The poverty that resulted from living on reservations with limited resources forced many Plains Indians to seek clothing and other supplies from charities. They changed the clothes they received in this way to suit their traditions. An example is the ribbon shirt, in which colored ribbons are sewn on a "cowboy" shirt in order to make a distinct article of Indian clothing.

Another way that Indian people adapted Western culture to fit their own is in the making of quilts. Northern Plains women are famous for their star quilts, which are bought as works of art by many non-Indians. Missionaries once taught Native

Blackfeet residence with sweat lodge and canvas lodge in foreground, Blackfeet Reservation, Montana.

women to quilt and introduced the eight-point star pattern. Today the star quilt has become a distinctive Plains design. These quilts are also used as gifts in traditional giveaway ceremonies, powwows, and other occasions such as funerals among the Northern Cheyenne.

Reservation Life

Once on the reservations, many Indian peoples attempted to become farmers. But most were unable to harvest enough to live on, because much of the land was not fertile. Indians lacked the money to purchase farm equipment and were unable to borrow money

from the bank. Large-scale commercial farming was therefore impossible.

As an alternative, the U.S. government encouraged cattle ranching. Some groups were successful cattle ranchers, such as the Blackfeet who registered over four hundred brands of cattle by the year 1900. Cattle buyers in Chicago purchased animals from both the Blackfeet and Northern Cheyenne reservations.

Many Plains Indians consider their early success with cattle to be a high point in their economic history. Today only a small percentage of reservation Indians make money this way. For example, on the Northern

Mosquito Run, Milk River Indian Days, August 1986.

Cheyenne reservation only 10 percent of families make a living by cattle ranching.

The Dawes General Allotment Act of 1887 divided reservation lands into 40 160-acre tracts for individual tribal members. Allotment made it even more difficult for Indians to support themselves off the land. [Also see U.S. Native American Populations and Their Lands chapter.] Because of allotment, most Plains Indians were especially hard hit by the agricultural depression after World War I (1914-18).

By 1930, government aid was necessary. Direct aid and work programs were put into place. However, these work programs ended when America entered World War II in 1941. Many jobless workers either entered the armed services or found jobs in war-related industries, many in urban areas.

After World War II ended in 1945, many Plains men and women returned to their reservations determined to improve their communities. Leaders became more vocal in demanding greater self-determination and control over reservation resources. Native leaders also wanted equal rights with other citizens and demanded that Congress repeal unfair laws. One law, for example, had been in place that banned the sale of alcohol to Indians. In 1952, this ban was lifted. After that reservation governments decided whether or not alcohol would be sold on their lands.

After World War II, the rest of America experienced new wealth, but on the reservations poverty increased. In the 1960s, America's "War on Poverty" gave tribal governments some opportunities to improve their standard of living. Most of the gains were short-term, however. More importantly, the political climate of the 1960s produced the Red Power movement and the American Indian Movement (AIM). [Also see Activism chapter.] These movements pushed for civil rights, greater cultural awareness, and Indian self-determination.

In order to generate income, some tribes whose reservations were rich in natural resources began to sell coal and oil and to lease mineral rights. These efforts, as well as other economic developments, provided limited relief on the reservations, but Plains reservations are still some of the poorest communities in the United States. The unemployment rate on the Northern Cheyenne reservation has been as high as 80 percent. In an effort to improve the reservations, tribal leaders have assumed greater control over the education of children. Many schools now emphasize Native cultures and help prepare children to participate in the reservation community. On the Plains a large number of tribally controlled community colleges have been established.

Today, Plains cultures are enjoying a revival of tradition on the reservations as tribal members continue to attend powwows, tribal fairs, Sun Dances, sweat ceremonies, and naming ceremonies. Many powwows are sacred dances, and are not open to public display. The Sun Dance has been revived and adapted. Traditional giveaway ceremonies are featured at many powwows. The peyote religion (or Native American Church) also finds many converts among Plains peoples. Urban Indians maintain their cultural ties by returning to the reservations for visits and special occasions, or by participating in tribal activities at social centers in the cities.

7
Native Groups of the Northwest Coast

Major Culture Areas

FACT FOCUS

- Salmon is the central food source on much of the Northwest Coast. In fact, some Northwest Coast groups today feel that a meal is not complete without at least a little salmon.
- The early European explorers in the Northwest Coast area were looking for the fabled Northwest Passage—an open sea passage that crossed North America.
- Because European traders were not interested in doing much trade in the Northwest Coast regions until the late 1700s, significant European settlement did not begin there until the 1790s.
- Many Northwest Coast groups combined Christianity and other European religions with their traditional religious beliefs to form new religious movements.
- In 1884, the Indian Act in Canada outlawed the potlatch, an important and widespread form of ceremonial feast central to the cultures of the Northwest Coast.

[See Chapter 3: Native Groups of the Northeast for an introduction to the study of major culture areas.]

Diverse Populations of the Northwest Coast

The many different groups of Northwest Coast peoples live in southeast Alaska and western parts of British Columbia, Washington, and Oregon. They have distinct cultures and speak a variety of languages.

The Tlingit homelands are in southeast Alaska. There they fished for salmon, but also harvested halibut, seal, and other sea animals. Tlingit villages were usually large, compared to other Northwest Coast tribes. The mountainous shores and rugged off-

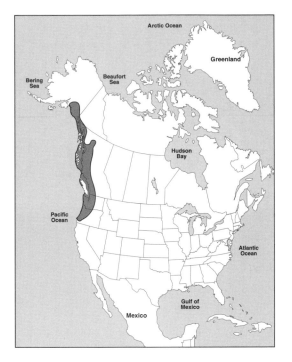

The Northwest Coast (shaded).

shore islands of southeast Alaska were home to about 15,000 Tlingit when the Europeans arrived in the late 1700s.

Just to the south of the Tlingit are the Haida. The Haida live in the southern part of Prince of Wales Island in Southeast Alaska and the Queen Charlotte Islands in British Columbia. They are well known along the coast for their woodworking skills, especially large totem poles and huge seaworthy canoes. In the late 1700s, the Haida numbered about 14,000.

The Tsimshian live on the north-central coast of British Columbia and inland in the Nass and Skeena River valleys. Along with the Tlingit and Haida, they are sometimes called the "northern matrilineal tribes" because of the way their societies are organized. In matrilineal societies, names and inheritances are passed down through the mother's side of the family rather than the

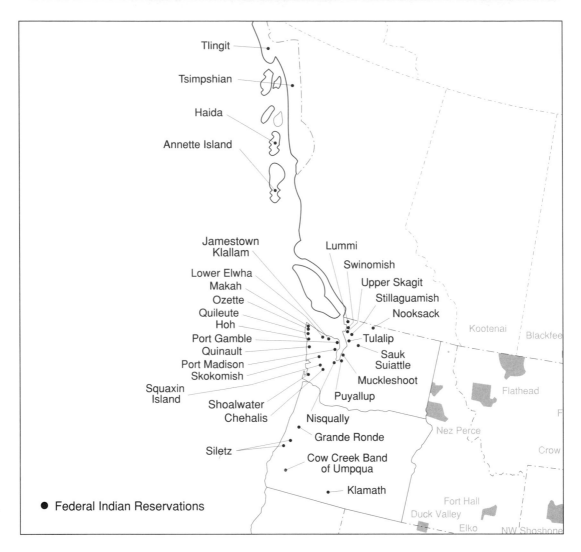

Contemporary Northwest Coast Indian tribes.

father's. The Tsimshian numbered about 14,500 in the late 1700s.

Among the Tlingit, Haida, and Tsimshian, society was divided into two **moieties** (or halves)—the Eagle and the Raven—which had its own rules and functions. Within each moiety were numerous clans, which had their own territories, histories, and characteristics. The clan was composed of several houses, and each house was run by a "master of the house"—usually a maternal or great uncle. Houses had their own plots of land, names, and crests. A house's crest was a picture, something like the European coat of arms, that displayed the history of the clan and the house.

Each clan and house had a particular rank or status based on wealth. Owning material goods, including slaves, crests, blankets, and totems, contributed to status. Also, generosity, skill in making speeches, and past accomplishments determined the position of the house or clan.

Clans and houses had rights to specific areas for fishing, berry picking, and hunting. Anyone could use an area, as long as they asked permission. Areas between each territory were open to everyone.

The **potlatch** was a central feature of these southeastern Alaska cultures. A potlatch was a ceremonial feast involving performances and the giving away of valuable gifts. These gifts were given to honor an individual, to strengthen relationships, to display one's generosity, and to honor the memory of those who had passed away.

Moving farther south, various bands of Native people who speak Kwakawala are found along the south-central coast of British Columbia and nearby eastern shores of Vancouver Island. These bands can be divided into northern and southern groups. The northern groups include the Haisla, Haihais, Bella Bella, and Owekeeno. The southern groups are known altogether as the Kwakiutl (or Kwakwaka'wakw). The Kwakiutl are famous for their extravagant potlatch ceremonies, as well as for other types of religious and secular ceremonies. At the time of European contact, the northern groups numbered about 7,500 and the southern groups about 19,000.

The west coast of Vancouver Island was home to the Nuu-Chah-Nulth (formerly known as Nootka). Along with the Makah, who lived in present-day Washington state, the Nuu-Chah-Nulth were well known as whalers and deep-sea navigators. One of the Nuu-Chah-Nulth bands was host to the first European settlement on the Northwest Coast. These bands totaled about 10,000 at the time of contact.

The Coast Salish consist of more than 36 distinct tribes and bands. They live in southwest British Columbia, southeast Vancouver Island, and western Washington. Two groups, the Bella Coola and the Tillamook, make up the largest number of Salish-speaking tribes in the area. The rest of the Coast Salish can be divided into four main groupings, based on language, culture, and area of residence. Altogether, the Coast Salish numbered about 45,500 in the late 1700s.

The Chinook inhabited the lower Columbia River from the Cascade Mountains to the Pacific Ocean. They controlled the waterways into the interior and were excellent traders, covering a wide area. In addition, the Chinook realized the potential of the enormous Columbia River salmon runs. They numbered about 10,500 in the mid-1700s; by 1850 their population was reduced to just a few hundred.

Numerous bands of tribes lived along the Oregon Coast and in the Willamette River Valley. These groups spoke various languages, such as Athapaskan and Penutian. Their cultures shared characteristics with both the Northwest Coast tribes to their north and the California cultures to their

The inside of a house in Nootka Sound, from the Cook Expedition, 1778.

south. In all, they numbered as many as 30,000 people in the 1700s.

Similarities and Differences among the Cultures

The most striking thing about the Northwest Coast area may be the many differences in language and culture which are found from the northern to southern areas. Even so, there are some characteristics shared by these groups.

Housing

The typical house of the Northwest Coast Indians was the longhouse. It was large and sheltered several families who were related in some way. Among the northern matrilineal groups, they were related through the female side of the family. Among the other groups, they were related through either the male or female side of the family. Inside the longhouse each family had its own partitioned area. Central fires burned for heat and light, but each family cooked its own meals and ate separately. Families could change houses if they wished.

Sometimes families separated in the summer months while they obtained the goods that supported them throughout the year. In winter the longhouse served as a ceremonial center and partitions were taken down to make room for guests and for dances.

Food Resources

Salmon was the most abundant and reliable source of food in the Northwest Coast area. Five species of salmon spent their

Johnnie Saux, a Quinaielt, holding a dog salmon, Taholah, Washington, 1936.

adult lives in the waters of the Pacific Ocean, traveling up the freshwater streams along the coast to spawn (lay their eggs). Native people caught large numbers of salmon in or near the freshwater streams with traps, nets, and **weirs.** A weir is a barricade placed across a stream to divert the salmon into a trap. Some fishing was also done in the salt waters. Although some salmon fishing took place throughout the year, most was done in the spring and fall. Family groups returned to specific locations each year.

While the men worked the traps, the women filleted the fish. The filleted fish were then preserved, either by being hung on a rack to be dried out by the winds, or hung in the rafters of the longhouse to be dried by the slow-burning fires. Some groups preserved as much as five hundred pounds of fish per person each year! To this day, some Native people feel that a meal is not complete without at least a little salmon.

Although salmon was the main food source for Northwest Coast Indians, they also caught many other types of fish, including clams, mussels, oysters, herring, halibut, and rockfish. The Tsimshian harvested tons of a small fish known as oolichan, which was rendered into oil. Oolichan was eaten as well as traded.

Marine animals such as seals, porpoise, and whales were also harvested. The Nuu-Chah-Nulth, Makah, and Quileute were all expert whalers. They hunted these large animals from dugout canoes, using hand-thrown spears. Some groups looked for whales that had beached or drifted to shore. But the Makah, Huu-Chah-Nulth, and Quileute would pursue the whales for days on end, often far out at sea. Their catch meant an important source of food, but also brought the status and prestige of being a successful whaler.

Northwest Coast Indians also hunted land mammals such as deer, elk, bear, and mountain goats. Individual hunters might hunt the animals, or groups would drive them into nets or ambushes. Hunting was more often done by groups who lived inland.

Mountain goats were valued for their horns, which were made into spoons and other tools. They also provided wool, which was spun into yarn and then woven into blankets. Some women also kept a type of small dog that could be shorn like a sheep. Its woolly fur was then spun into yarn.

Gathering plant foods began in the spring, but was mostly done during the late summer and early fall. Starchy tubers such as camas and wapato and broken fern roots were harvested in abundance. In some cases, these plants were grown on plots owned by family groups. Berries and other fruits were also plentiful, and they were eaten fresh or dried for later use.

Culture

Because the Northwest Coast people lived in large, settled groups and had abundant supplies of food, they were able to support some members as full-time or part-time artisans. Weavers, basket makers, wood carvers, and stone workers spent many hours making their handiwork.

Winter months were busy with ceremonial activities. Spirit dances, ceremonial performances, masked dances, and the most famous ceremony of all—the potlatch— were held. Potlatching was a way for an individual to express his social standing in the community. His position was reinforced and increased by giving away gifts and feasting with guests. Potlatching may have increased in the 1800s because of the increase of luxury items and trade goods brought in by Europeans and other traders.

European Contact

The earliest European explorers in the Northwest Coast area, such as John Cabot who sailed from England in 1497, were looking for the fabled Northwest Passage. They hoped to find this open sea passage across North America to make it easier to trade with far eastern empires. No such passage existed, but in their search for the Northwest Passage, Europeans reached the Northwest Coast in the late 1700s.

The first to arrive were the Spanish, followed by the Russians from the north. At first the Europeans found little reason to stay. Some trade took place aboard the ships, but the area was not rich in furs and the Natives were hard bargainers. Soon, however, sea otter pelts began to bring in high prices in China, and a lively trade developed.

In 1789, the Spanish established a post at Nootka Sound on Vancouver Island, and the struggle for control of trade began. The Russians, Spanish, British, and Americans all joined the fray, but the Native people were unconcerned with these struggles as long as they could buy manufactured goods. Trade goods made the Natives' work easier and increased their wealth.

Through the late 1800s, non-Native settlement of the Northwest Coast progressed at a staggering rate. During this settlement period, treaties were signed with the United States, reservation communities were established in British Columbia, and the number of Native villages in Alaska shrank to a few. At this time, the Native population rapidly declined because of European diseases for which the Native peoples had no immunity. By 1900 non-Natives outnumbered Natives in most areas, and the Native societies were overtaken by the growing dominant society.

New religious expressions arose early in the settlement period. Traditional spiritualism and practices continued. **Shamans**— people who understood supernatural matters and performed in rituals—were consulted to cure the sick, foresee the future, and help in hunting and other activites. Christianity also attracted many converts. New movements also arose that were a combination of Native American religions and Christianity or other beliefs. Today in Northwest Coast Indian communities there are a number of Christians as well as Shakers (members of a religious movement begun in England in the mid-1700s. Shakers lived in communes and practiced self-denial and strict spiritual discipline).

As non-Natives controlled more of the area, Northwest Coast peoples found it difficult to continue to fish, hunt, and gather as they had before. Fishing, logging, and farming became the area's main economic activities. Conflicts over uses of the land arose between Natives and non-Natives. As traditional activities and resources became limited, Native people sought wage labor in nearby non-Native communities. Because of growing poverty on the reservations, many Native people chose to leave the reservations, an act encouraged by government policy.

Contemporary Life

Today many Northwest Coast Native American communities appear to be the same as their non-Native neighbors. But behind the familiar trappings is a foundation of Native life that has remained and adapted to modern ways. For example, multi-family longhouses were abandoned in most areas by 1900. Yet the strong ties of kinship that were part of longhouse life have continued. Extended family groups depend on each other in time of need, to help with potlatches, or to support one another in struggling for political power.

Nooksack tribal gathering and salmon bake to discuss fishing rights, Deming, Washington, 1970.

Many changes have occurred over the past one hundred years. Because Native people in the Northwest Coast area have lived under different governments and influences, changes are best seen by looking at three main areas: Alaska, British Columbia, and western Washington and Oregon.

Alaska

Until 1867, Alaska was part of Russia. The Tlingit and some of the Haida were fairly isolated, and even after the United States acquired Alaska, contact with outsiders was minimal. The Alaska Gold Rush in the 1890s changed this situation rapidly. Settlers flooded in, and Native people began to find work as fishers and loggers and in other jobs. Many adopted Christianity. Formal education became widespread.

Interest in Alaska's resources continued to grow, especially when oil was discovered soon after Alaska became a state in 1959. Conflicts arose over ownership of land and other rights. To resolve these conflicts, the Alaska Native Claims Settlement Act was passed in 1971. Through this act, Alaska Natives selected certain lands. In exchange they gave up title to the rest of Alaska.

They also received federal money to establish corporations to be run by Native Americans. Alaska Natives organized into 12 corporations and these corporations have since become their primary political groups, and wield a lot of power and influence. Free of the limitations of reservation life, the Tlingit and Haida have prospered.

British Columbia

The Native people in British Columbia live in remote areas and work in logging, commercial fishing, and other occupations. The Natives of British Columbia have never signed treaties with the Canadian government. Instead of treaties, British Columbia set up a system of **reserves,** planning to set aside Native peoples' lands until they became assimilated into the dominant society.

The Indian Act, passed in 1884 and revised several times since, was the basis of Native policy in Canada. With special attention to the Northwest Coast, the Indian Act outlawed the potlatch. Officials were not able to enforce this law until the 1920s, however, and even then potlatching never disappeared completely—it just went under-

Puyallup Indian arrested for protesting violation of treaty fishing rights.

ground for many years. Potlatching was revived publicly in 1951 when the potlatch law was abolished.

Since the 1880s, Native leaders in British Columbia have made efforts to gain rights to land and resources. It was not until the 1970s that visible results of these important efforts began to appear. Even now there is no clear direction on how claims should be handled. Many end up in the courts for decades.

Western Washington and Oregon

In the mid-1850s, tribes in Western Washington and Oregon entered into treaties with the United States. The treaties established reservations and gave Native Americans certain rights, including fishing rights.

After World War II the United States began to "terminate" or end the special relationship it had with Native American groups under treaty and law. Many Native Americans were urged to relocate to cities in order to find work. Some reservations estimate that as many as one-third of their people were relocated during the 1950s. Most lived in poverty in the cities, and the loss of people was a drain on the reservation community. Today about 20,000 Native Americans live in Seattle.

Three Oregon tribes were terminated as a result of government policy: the Klamath, Siletz, and Grande Ronde. They sought to be reinstated as tribes almost immediately, because they found they could not survive as an intact community without the rights establis\hed by treaty. After nearly 30 years, this was granted.

The present policy of self-determination for Northwest Coast tribes gives them greater control over land, resources, and institutions such as education. The activism of Northwest Coast Indians that began in the 1960s and 1970s has been very important in restoring Native rights. A well-known example of this activism is the "fish-in" movement of the early 1970s. Because of the active protest of Native Americans, a 1974 court decision restored Native fishing rights to treaty tribes in western Washington. [Also see Activism chapter.] Native people now harvest 50 percent of all commercial salmon and make significant contributions to other fisheries. Also, Native Americans run hatcheries that release millions of salmon fry into the public waters each year.

8

Native Groups in Alaska

Major Culture Areas

[See Chapter 3: Native Groups in the Northeast for an introduction to the study of major culture areas.]

Traditional Alaska Life

The Aleut

The Aleut occupy the 1,400-mile-long Aleutian island chain, part of the Alaska peninsula, and the Pribilof Islands in the Bering Sea. This area is rich in resources, which enabled it to support the densest native population in Alaska (that is, the most people per square mile of land). At the time of the first Russian contact in the 1600s, there were about 16,000 Aleut.

The abundant sea life included sea urchins, clams, octopus, fish, sea otters, seals, and whales. These were used for food, clothing, and homes. Birds and their eggs, berries, wild rice, celery, and other plants were also part of the Aleut diet. The men were skilled hunters on the open sea, and used two-person skin boats (baidarka) for hunting seals and whales.

Aleutian villages were situated along the coast, allowing easy access to the sea. They were small, usually with only one hundred to two hundred inhabitants. Two to five families lived in houses called barabaras, which were built partly underground.

The family was the primary grouping in Aleut society, serving as the basis for social relations, **economics** (the way people supported themselves and accumulated wealth),

Alaska (shaded).

The Inuit and Yupik

Yupik and Inuit peoples live in a large area with many different environments: in the mountain ranges and deep fjords (narrow inlets of the sea set between high cliffs) in the south; in the windswept mountains of the Alaskan peninsula; and in the tundra and flat lowlands of the Arctic province. Yupik Eskimo is spoken in southwestern Alaska, and Inuit is spoken in an area to the north stretching across northern Canada to Greenland.

Early Yupik and Inuit societies focused on the continual search for food. Food resources included caribou and other land animals in the interior, whales and sea animals along the coasts, and fish in the southwestern areas. The Yupik and Inuit spent part of each year settled at a home base, and part of the year moving about in search of food. From 12 to 50 people might travel together.

Extended families were common, often composed of three or four generations. Families were fairly equal and independent. They would often share with others, intermarry, and hunt together. There was consid-

warfare, and political relations. Aleuts were a matrilineal society, with inheritance following the mother's line of relatives. Children were trained and disciplined by the mother's family. Men were responsible for hunting and the care of tools and boats. Women cared for the home and gathered food along the beaches and shallow waters.

Traditional society was loosely divided between nobles, commoners, and slaves captured in wars with other villages. The most respected hunters, those with years of experience and great skill, became Aleut chiefs. However, chiefs had little real power and decisions required the agreement of everyone. Warfare was not uncommon among Aleut groups. Wars were fought for a variety of reasons—revenge, to gain slaves, or for trade.

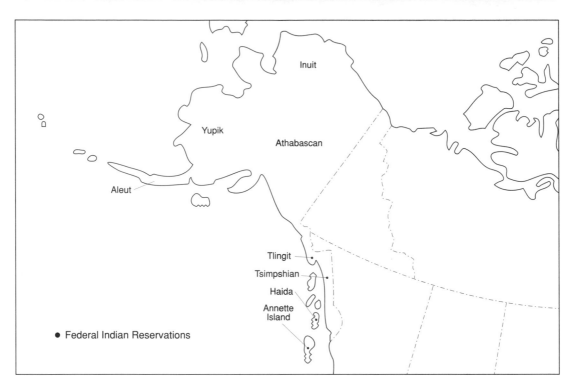

Contemporary Alaska Native tribes.

erable conflict, however, between different groups. Strangers with no specific reason for being in an area were in great danger. Within each family, people were divided by age and gender (whether male or female). At the head was the boss, or umialik. Leaders were usually those who showed great skill or courage, and who would be able to foresee future problems.

Shamans, or spiritual leaders, were also powerful because of their connection with the spirit world, their ability to cure people, and their knowledge. Every settlement had a gathering place, called a gargi, where people met for conversation and ritual. [Also see Canada's Native Peoples and Their Lands chapter.]

The Northern Athapaskan

The northern Athapaskan (or Athabascan) lived in a large area extending through most of the interior of Alaska, bordered by the Arctic to the north and the temperate forests to the south. The northern Athapaskan included six groups: the Ingalik, Koyukon, Tanana, Tanaina, Ahtna, and Upper Tanana.

Although these groups were not actual tribes, they occupied their own territories. Within each territory were smaller bands. These bands lived together part of the year, and then separated to follow the migrations of animals for fishing and hunting. Bands were composed of people related by blood or by marriage.

Interior of an Inuit house.

Men formed hunting partnerships; one man killed the animal and the other distributed it. Resources were always shared. Because people needed to be able to move about in search of food, owning material goods was not necessary or even practical.

The Athapaskans practiced "strategic hunting." Working together, they would direct fish into weirs (special barricade traps), corral caribou, or catch waterfowl in their breeding grounds.

Traditional Native societies were complex and well adapted to the physical environment. Alaska Natives were connected to each other in an intricate system of relations that governed whom they could marry, where the couple would live, where their fishing and hunting places would be, and who would be the leader of the group. The success of Alaskan Native social systems also depended on a number of other factors. Natural disasters, population growth, or interference from outsiders could easily upset the balance of their societies.

Russian Colonialism

The Russians were the first outsiders to contact Native Alaskans in the first half of the 1700s. Wanting to make a profit from the sale of sea otter and seal skins, Siberian fur hunters launched expeditions to the area. In 1766 the Russians declared control over the Aleutians, but in fact there was little government control over Russian traders and hunters. The Russians brought epidemic diseases to the native people, who had no immunity and usually died rather than simply becoming ill. Many others were murdered. It is estimated that 90 percent of the native population was lost to disease or murder.

Those who survived were often forced into slave labor. The Russians used the men as hunters on the open sea, or as warriors as they moved into eastern Alaska. However, the Russians stayed mostly on the coast. They went into the interior on occasion, but hostile tribes, severe cold weather, and difficulty in moving over the land limited their expansion. By 1867, when the United States acquired Alaska, the Russians ruled only a small portion of it.

American Colonialism

U.S. expansion into Alaska was motivated by fur and, more importantly, gold. Although Congress had passed laws to protect Native lands, there was little to prevent non-Natives from building there. Fish canneries, gold mining camps, trade and manufacturing sites, railroads, timber harvesting, homesteads, towns—all came to Alaska in the late 1800s and early 1900s.

During World War II, U.S. leaders became aware of how important Alaska was in terms of defense. In 1959, President Eisenhower proclaimed Alaska the forty-ninth state.

Land Claims

The influx of people and money to Alaska during the 1900s caused conflict among Native peoples, and they soon prepared an opposition movement. Often they were not consulted when major projects were planned on or near their lands. For example, the U.S. Atomic Energy Commission gave permission to use 1,600 square miles around Point Hope (an Inuit village) for a nuclear explosion. This explosion was to create a deep water port on the northwestern coast of Alaska.

Alaska Natives organized to prevent any more of these situations and to protect their rights. By 1967 they had formed 12 regional associations to pursue land claims. The regional leaders then formed the Alaska Federation of Natives (AFN). The purpose of the AFN was to protect Native rights, inform the public about Native issues, preserve Native culture and values, and try to settle land claims.

The Alaska Native Claims Settlement Act, 1971

The first major bill to settle land claims in

Salmon drying. Aleut village, Old Harbor, Alaska, 1889.

Alaska was passed in 1971. Oil companies wanted to build a pipeline across Native lands to carry oil south, Alaska Natives wanted their land, and conservationists wanted to preserve wilderness areas. To settle this and other such issues, the Alaska Native Claims Settlement Act (ANCSA) was signed into law in 1971. Alaska Natives received $962 million and 44 million acres of land. In exchange, they gave up title to the rest of their lands in Alaska.

ANCSA cleared the path for the construction of the pipeline. It also set aside millions of acres of public lands for parks and wilderness areas. In the end, 12 percent of Alaska will be privately owned by Native peoples, 28 percent will be owned by the state of Alaska, and 59 percent by the federal government.

The ANCSA also resulted in the formation of 12 regional corporations to be in charge of economic development and land use. It was assumed that these profit-making corporations would lead to an improved standard of living for Alaska Natives.

Social and Economic Profile of Alaska Natives

There are over 100,000 Alaska Natives in the United States. About 85,600 live in Alaska: 44,000 are Yupik or Inuit; 31,000

Inuit Children, Barrow, Alaska.

are Athapaskan, Tlingit, Haida, or Tsimshian; and 10,000 are Aleut. The total number of Alaska Natives is growing rapidly. During the 1980s, the Inuit and Yupik population grew by 30 percent, the Aleut by 24 percent, and the other groups by 43 percent.

In spite of these increases, however, there is a steady decline in the percentage of the Alaska population that is Native. In 1950, 26 percent of Alaska's population was Native; by 1990 only 15.6 percent were Native people. Still, Natives are the majority in five regions of Alaska, including the Arctic Slope and Bering Strait.

The majority of Native Alaskans (56 percent) live in small villages ranging in size from 50 to 900 people. The average Native family has four children. There have been improvements in the lives of Native Alaskans over the past 20 years in health,

education, and employment. Living conditions have also improved; the majority of houses now have indoor plumbing, phones, and sewer and water outlets.

However, poverty is still a problem for Alaska Natives. More than 25 percent of the Native population lives below the official poverty level. Twice as many Natives as non-Natives are out of work. The average income for a Native family is about half of the average income for a non-Native family in Alaska.

Statistics indicate that Alaska Natives have difficult lives. They die from violent causes—such as accidents, murder, suicide, and alcoholism—at a much higher rate than the general population. Native suicide and murder rates are four times the U.S. average. Among young men 20 to 24 years old, the suicide rate is 20 times the national average.

Self-Determination and the Future

Alaska Natives try to retain their rights and ability to govern themselves in three major ways: 1) by improving and protecting their ability to produce what they need to live on and maintain a **subsistence economy**; 2) through economic development of their villages and regions; and 3) by making their tribal governments stronger.

Most Alaska Natives rely on subsistence economy to some extent. In other words, they rely on food or other products that they grow, catch, or make for their own use. In rural areas, Native people produce more than 50 percent of their food. Clothing, heating, housing, and arts and crafts are also supported by subsistence activities. Native leaders are actively working to protect the ability of their people to support themselves in this way. Therefore, fishing and hunting rights are particularly important issues.

Although corporations were formed to increase the standard of living for Alaska Natives and their communities, the results have had little impact on the day-to-day lives of most Native people. Only a small number of people has prospered as a result of economic development.

Many Alaska Natives look to their tribal governments for solutions to their problems.

There remains some confusion over how much authority and independence tribal governments actually have. Laws and court decisions are often contradictory. Still, village councils continue to operate tribal courts, claim control over their land and resources, and work to determine the direction their communities will take. Most are confident that their efforts will lead to improvements in the future.

9

Native Groups
of Oklahoma

Major Culture Areas

FACT FOCUS

- Oklahoma was once called "Indian Territory." In the early 1800s, while relocating many tribes there, the U.S. government had plans to make the area into an Indian commonwealth, governed by a confederacy of tribes.
- When Oklahoma became a state in 1907, all hope for a free Indian state there was lost.
- There are 600,000 Native Americans in Oklahoma, more than in any other state.
- Oklahoma's Red Earth celebration each June is the largest Indian celebration in the world.

[See Chapter 3: Native Groups in the Northeast for an introduction to the study of major culture areas.]

Indian Territory

The land that now forms most of the state of Oklahoma appears as "Indian Territory" on maps drawn in the 1800s. Today, Oklahoma has the largest number of Indian people and the most tribes of any state in the United States. The state is truly the "Home of the Red People," as Chief Allen Wright has freely translated the Choctaw name, Okla Homma.

More than 67 tribes exist in Oklahoma, and 29 of these are federally recognized Indian Nations. Interestingly, only a few of these tribes (probably less than six) lived in Oklahoma before European contact. The major reason Indians settled in Oklahoma was U.S. government policy.

Most Oklahoma Indian tribes were resettled in Oklahoma against their wishes during the 1800s. At that time, the policy of the

Oklahoma (shaded).

Oklahoma was admitted to the Union as the forty-sixth state.

The Trail of Tears

In the late 1820s and throughout the 1830s, the removal of Eastern Indians to Oklahoma began. The Five Civilized Tribes (the Choctaw, Chickasaw, Creek, Cherokee, and Seminole) were driven out of their homeland in the South. Their journey came to be known as "The Trail of Tears." Almost 60,000 members of these nations walked on foot over eight hundred miles. Poorly clothed and fed, forced to march even during winter months, from four to eight thousand Native Americans died on the Trail of Tears. In all the forced marches during this period, tens of thousands of Indians—up to one-third of those removed from their homes— perished.

Once resettled, the Five Tribes established governments in Oklahoma and ruled themselves relatively free of interference from the federal government. The Five Civilized Tribes were so named because in their homelands they had formed constitutional governments and school systems, and some had converted to Christianity. In their new home, the Five Tribes quickly established new governments, schools, and community programs. In fact, they achieved a level of literacy (ability to read and write) that was higher than that of their non-Native neighbors.

Before the Civil War, the Quapaw, Seneca, Shawnee, and other tribes were also moved to Oklahoma. Eventually, over 60 tribes were relocated there. Once settled in Oklahoma, many Indians found it to be a quiet haven. Eventually, they came to love the land. Many freely practiced their tribal traditions and prospered.

U.S. government was to remove all Indians from their homelands and settle them in the West. There was a proposed companion policy to removal during President Andrew Jackson's administration (1830-38). Oklahoma was to be established as an Indian commonwealth or territory and governed by a confederation of tribes. The proposal never passed into action, but under treaty, this new land was to be set aside solely for Indian use—no non-Indians were to be allowed to settle in their midst.

Gradually, however, Indian lands shrank as federal policy and failure to protect Indian rights allowed non-Native settlers to take over Indian territories. Finally, in 1907,

Ponca Indian powwow near Ponca City, Oklahoma.

After the Civil War, many other Indian groups (such as the Comanche, Kiowa, Cheyenne, and Apache) were moved to Indian Territory. In addition, thousands of non-Native settlers moved in illegally. Indian Territory became notorious for the bandits and killers that drifted in. Trying to maintain law and order, Congress established a special federal court for Indian Territory. This court was headed by Isaac C. Parker, known as the "Hanging Judge."

Government policy greatly reduced the land holdings of Native peoples. The Dawes General Allotment Act of 1887 divided up Indian lands. The Curtis Act of 1898 abolished tribal governments. In 1889, the famous Oklahoma land runs opened the territory to non-Natives. These were spectacular one-day chances to acquire former Indian lands. Combined, these actions caused the loss of most Indian lands that were fertile or mineral rich.

The New State of Oklahoma

In 1890, the Oklahoma Organic Act reduced Indian Territory to the eastern portion of the territory. The act created Oklahoma Territory in the western portion, and there established a U.S. territorial government.

Decades of conflict over efforts of the U.S. government to make Indian Territory

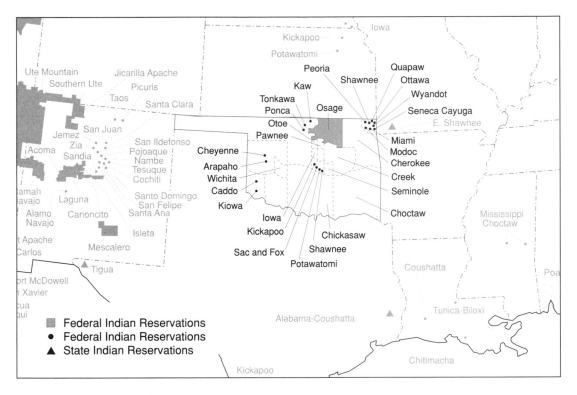

Contemporary Oklahoma Indian tribes.

into a state resulted in Oklahoma's statehood in 1907. The promise of a free Indian state had dissolved.

It may not be possible for non-Indians to understand the depth of the Oklahoma Indians' grief over the loss of their nationhood. In the *Chronicles of Oklahoma 26,* Edward E. Dale described a Cherokee woman's reaction. The woman refused to attend the statehood ceremonies with her husband, who was a non-Indian. He returned and said to her: "Well, Mary, we no longer live in the Cherokee Nation. All of us are now citizens of the state of Oklahoma." Thirty years later as she recalled that day, tears came to her eyes. "It broke my heart. I went to bed and cried all night long. It seemed more than I could bear that the Cherokee Nation, my country and my people's country, was no more."

Since Oklahoma became a state, Indian tribes have kept their status as self-governing and independent communities, except for limitations placed on them by treaties, agreements, or laws. Oklahoma Indians have the lowest income level and the highest unemployment rate of any group in Oklahoma.

Once, the Indians owned all the land in the state, but now they have a greatly reduced land base. At the turn of the century, the Five Tribes owned 19.5 million acres of land. By 1975 Oklahoma tribal lands had shrunk to a mere 65,000 acres, and individ-

Choctaw Council House, Tuskahoma, Oklahoma.

ual Native Americans owned about one million acres of land.

Today, as many as 600,000 present-day Oklahomans identify themselves as Indians more than in any other state. In a 65-mile radius around Tulsa, there is the highest non-reservation population of Indians anywhere in the world.

Oklahoma Indians have shared the unique experience of having been forcibly relocated. They have adapted in ways which have shaped their sense of Indian identity today. Beginning in the early 1800s, there is a history of tribal cooperation among the Indian groups in Oklahoma. Councils and meetings helped to reduce conflict and produce unified action to solve common problems.

Like many other Native Americans, Oklahoma Indians are currently experiencing a revival of the traditions they and their ancestors fought so hard to maintain. Thousands of Oklahoma Indians living outside the state plan their vacations to come home for tribal celebrations, with powwows and gourd dances, rodeos and competitions. Oklahoma's Red Earth celebration in June is now the largest Indian celebration in the world.

10

Native Groups of the Plateau, Great Basin, and Rocky Mountains

Major Culture Areas

FACT FOCUS

- Great Basin, Plateau, and Rocky Mountain Indians, little bothered by settlers before 1843, gave explorers Lewis and Clark an extremely warm reception and a lot of help in their travels in the early 1800s.
- In 1843 the Oregon Trail opened, crossing Idaho and Oregon, and within ten years the government began placing Native peoples on reservations.
- Wovoka, the son of a Paiute shaman, initiated the second Ghost Dance movement after having a vision from the Great Spirit in 1889.

[See Chapter 3: Native Groups in the Northeast for an introduction to the study of major culture areas.]

Numerous Indian communities continue to live today in their ancestral homelands on the Columbia Plateau of eastern Oregon and Washington state, in the Great Basin, and in the Rocky Mountains. In these regions, the Indian nations share many cultural traditions. All of the tribes enjoy a rich oral tradition about their history and origins and they share a deep respect for the earth, which supports them with rich food resources of roots, berries, game, and fish.

The Lewis and Clark Expedition

In the first years of the 1800s, Indians living in present-day Oregon, Washington, Idaho, and Montana met the expedition of American explorers Meriwether Lewis and

Plateau, Great Basin, and Rocky Mountains (shaded).

William Clark. Sacagawea, the long-lost sister of the Shoshoni chief Kameawaite, helped lead Lewis and Clark to Great Falls, Montana. Kameawaite then led the expedition to present-day western Montana. From there the Flathead Indians led them westward across Idaho.

When Lewis and Clark entered the lands of the Nez Percé, they found helpful scouts, food, and canoes to continue their journey to the Pacific Ocean. When they reached the Palouse village of Quosispah, they were greeted with celebrations and singing.

Several tribes, including the Yakima, Wishram, Walla Walla, and Cayuse, sent representatives to meet the U.S. explorers.

Relations between the explorers and Native peoples were friendly. They traded goods, and Lewis and Clark honored some of the chiefs with medals bearing the words "peace" and "friendship."

Upon their return, Lewis and Clark reported the many wondrous things they had seen, including vast numbers of fur-bearing animals. The United States claimed the entire Northwest as their territory, and encouraged others to relocate to the region.

European Settlement

Less than a year later (by 1810) British traders traveled through the area, and soon three major fur-trading companies set up trading posts or factories in the Northwest. These were the Northwest Company, the American Fur Company, and the Hudson's Bay Company. The traders were eager to take advantage of the furs and horses provided by the Indians.

In 1843, the Oregon Trail was opened from Idaho across Oregon to the Grande

Family of Bannocks in front of a grass tent, Idaho, 1872.

Ronde Valley. Soon many settlers used the Oregon Trail to travel to the Pacific Northwest Coast. The newcomers established territorial governments in present-day Washington and Oregon, and asserted political power over the Native peoples.

Diseases brought by the settlers spread rapidly among the Indians, killing many. Tensions and conflict mounted. Soon after, the Gold Rush spread north from California into the plateau and mountains, and miners invaded. The gold miners showed little or no regard for the rights of the Indians.

Then the United States began to pay more attention to the area, and in 1853 created the Oregon Territory and the Washington Territory. United States policy toward Indians was focused on taking title to their lands, moving Indians onto reservations, and establishing military and civil power over the tribes. Over time, the U.S. took nearly all Indian land in the area, but not without a fight.

Contact with Great Basin peoples came relatively late—in the 1850s. Many of these peoples, who had lived by hunting animals and gathering roots and plants, went to work for U.S. ranchers and farmers. Many worked as cowboys driving cattle. Others worked at jobs such as planting, cultivating, and harvesting grains, or taking care of livestock.

The Ghost Dance

Many Indian nations in the West were concerned that their way of life was being threatened. Death from diseases brought by settlers was widespread. On the Plains the buffalo and other game were declining. In response to these concerns, the second Ghost Dance movement arose in 1890.

The first Ghost Dance movement swept west from Nevada into California in 1870. The second was initiated by Wovoka, the son of a Paiute shaman. Wovoka had a vision from the Great Spirit, and the Ghost Dance was revealed to him. The Ghost Dance included many Paiute traditions, such as the Round Dance, which was performed to achieve successful transition to the next world after death. In some versions, the dance was to help bring back to earth many dead ancestors and to replenish game. It was hoped that these rituals would restore Indians to their former, more prosperous condition before the invasion of non-Native settlers.

The Ghost Dance declined rapidly after the 1890 massacre of Sioux at Wounded Knee in South Dakota, where the Ghost Dance had

The prophet Wovoka (seated) in his later years.

been performed. Wovoka encouraged the Great Basin peoples to continue to follow the teachings he had received in a vision from the Great Spirit. He urged them to love one another and live in peace with everyone. His teachings were probably a mixture of his traditional beliefs and Christian thought, with which he was familiar.

Relocation

Gold was discovered in Oregon Territory in the mid-1800s. The U.S. Army responded to violence between miners and the Yakima Indians by sending troops, who invaded the lands of Walla Walla, Umatilla, Cayuse, and Palouse Indians. The resulting Plateau

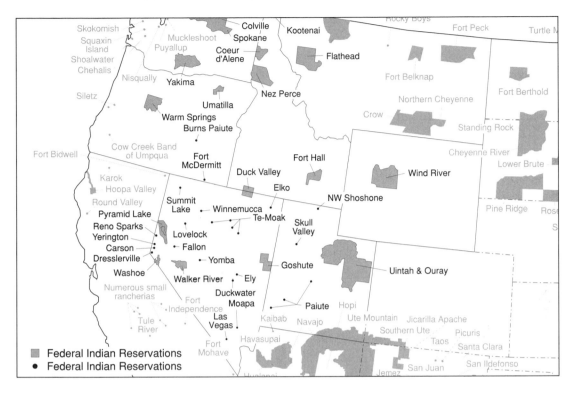

Contemporary Rocky Mountain Indian tribes.

Indian War brought the full powers of the government on many Plateau groups. Few of these people had been involved in the conflict, but the volunteer soldiers sought to punish all Indians.

In Idaho, the government had set up the Fort Hall reservation for a band of Shoshoni, but in the 1870s decided to place the Bannock Indians on the reservation as well. The government promised rations, but did not follow through, and many Shoshoni and Bannock at Fort Hall faced starvation. The Bureau of Indian Affairs (BIA) interfered with their efforts to hunt and gather off the reservation. A series of battles ensued and by June 1878, it had become a major military

conflict. Seven hundred Bannock and Paiute joined forces in southeastern Oregon to fight the Battle of Camp Curry. Afterward, the Bannock and Paiute moved north toward the Umatilla reservation in Oregon and U.S. forces returned the Shoshoni and Bannock to the Fort Hall reservation.

In the 1880s, reformers of American Indian policy decided that the trouble with Indians was that they held reservations communally and not individually. The reformers decided to break up reservations into individual lots so that Indians would have private lots to ranch and farm. U.S. policymakers reasoned that this land policy would enable Indians to become "civilized" because they would have a direct stake in their own economic livelihood. Most reformers, however, knew little about Indian cultures and practices, such as their methods of hunting, fishing, and gathering. Few, if any Indians in the plateau, mountain, or Great Basin regions farmed, and it would take years for them to alter their cultures to accommodate U.S. reformers. Life on reservations was hard. The people often became dependent on government rations, and most reservations could not adequately support their small Indian populations.

Congress passed the General Allotment Act in 1887, which called for the division of reservations into individual parcels of 160, 80, or 40 acres. Each Indian received an **allotment,** and the excess land was sold to non-Indian settlers. Between 1890 and 1914, the United States made 4,506 allotments on the Yakima reservation. Because many conservative Yakima refused to take allotments, 798,000 acres remained in tribal hands. Spokane tribal lands were divided in 1902. The government forced 651 tribe members to accept allotments totaling 65,750 acres. The remainder of the reservation was sold to non-Indian timber, agricultural, and ranching interests.

The Coeur d'Alene people of Idaho were granted an original reservation of 598,500 acres, for which they gave up 184,960 acres of their homelands. Government allotment of their lands from 1905 to 1909 left the Coeur d'Alene with only 51,040 acres of the lands they traditionally lived on. The Indians of the Flathead reservation in Montana originally controlled 1,242,969 acres of land. The government allotted land to 2,378 Indians and sold 404,047 acres to U.S. settlers. The state of Montana took another

60,843 acres and the United States kept 1,757 acres for itself. In 1910 the government opened the rest of the Flathead land for settlement.

During the nineteenth century smallpox, measles, and venereal (sexually transmitted) diseases killed thousands of Native Americans in the Columbia Plateau, Great Basin, and Rocky Mountain area. In the early twentieth century tuberculosis, influenza, and pneumonia killed thousands more. Not only life and lands were lost, but culture, language, and family life were losing ground to the Bureau of Indian Affairs' attempts to "civilize" Native Americans. One of the BIA's chief strategies to **assimilate** Indians (make them "blend in" with mainstream American society) was to force Native American children to go to reservation schools or boarding schools, where they were not allowed to speak their native languages or practice their religions.

The 1930s Indian Reorganization Act stopped some of the destruction of previous U.S. policies. It provided that Indians could form new governments of their own, with tribal laws and constitutions. It also allowed Indians to place allotted lands in trust so that they could not be sold. Some Indians accepted the Reorganization Act and others did not. The Indian Claims Commission was formed as a more effective way for Indians to sue the federal government for treaty violations. Several monetary awards were provided to Indians, after many years in the court system.

In the 1950s the U.S. government attempted to "terminate" its treaty and legal relationship with various tribes. One of the groups it wished to terminate was the Colville reserva-

Angelic La Moose, whose grandfather was a Flathead chief, wearing costume her mother made, standing in front of a tent, Flathead Reservation, Montana, 1913.

nomic development. Each year they sponsor workshops on cultural renewal, and they encourage their young people to participate in their annual Powwow and Circle Celebration held in Nespelem, Washington. The tribe owns a sawmill, a package log cabin sales business, and a trading post. Young people attend colleges and universities in the region, and some have returned to the reservation to share their skills with the community.

On the Flathead reservation, the Kutenai, (or Kootenai), Kalispel, and Flathead have begun a project to preserve their oral histories, languages, and songs. The Shoshoni and Bannock on the Fort Hall reservation are often employed in ranching, farming, and small businesses. The tribe owns farming and construction enterprises, and runs a 20,000-acre irrigation project that brings water to both Indians and non-Indians. The Shoshoni and Bannock run their own health center, adult education program, and youth recreation program.

Two of the most active tribes in the region are the Indians of the Warm Springs reservation in Oregon and the Yakima people of Washington. The Indians of the Warm Springs reservation run a logging operation and Warm Springs Forest Products Industries, which includes a sawmill and a plywood plant. They built and operate a resort and convention center called Kah-Nee-Ta, which has generated money used for health and education programs.

Warm Springs Indians have herds of wild horses, which they sell. They also manage a salmon hatchery. In 1982, the tribe became the first in the United States to open its own hydroelectric plant. Along with this economic success, the people of Warm Springs

tion in Washington state. Colville tribal members who lived off the reservation favored termination because it would bring them a cash settlement. Tribal members living on the reservation opposed it because it would end important treaty rights and threatened to break up Indian cultures and communities. Although there was a division among tribal members for several years, the Colville tribe never agreed to termination.

The Colville tribe has since made significant strides in health, education, and eco-

reservations have maintained their traditional beliefs through the Washani religion—a faith shared by many Indians on the Yakima reservation as well.

The Yakima tribe manages its own forest products industry and operates a furniture manufacturing plant. They also manage 2.7 million acres of rangeland and 150,000 acres of farmland. The Yakima control their own water through the Wapato Project. They have also developed small businesses and banking and fishing enterprises.

With their income the Yakima have funded a major housing project and an extensive tribal cultural center. Shaped like a longhouse, the center contains a library, museum, gift shop, theater, restaurant, and office space. The Yakima place great value on education and offer scholarships to young people. They also help to prepare students for college with a summer educational program. Each year the Yakima support numerous powwows and festivals to celebrate their Indian heritage.

Programs for teaching Indian languages began in the 1970s and continue in the 1990s on several reservations, including the Colville, Umatilla, Nez Percé, Coeur d'Alene, Spokane, and Yakima. Native Americans of the regions consider preserving language to be one of their most important projects.

Fishing rights are one of the most important issues facing the Indians of the plateau and eastern mountain region. They have protested the destruction of the salmon, and they have fought for their treaty rights to fish, hunt, graze, and gather in their usual places—both on and off the reservation. The struggle for fishing rights continues to be an issue for Native Americans and for those who support their rights. In fact, fishing rights became a campaign issue during the race for governor of Washington in 1992.

11

Native Groups
of California

Major Culture Areas

FACT FOCUS

- There were as many as 340,000 Native peoples in California in 1540. By 1900 there were only 18,000 left, a loss of about 95 percent. In 1993, however, about 200,000 Indians lived in the state.
- Beginning in 1769, the Spanish built a series of 23 missions in California in which they virtually enslaved thousands of Native Californians for about 65 years.
- Native laborers forced to work in Spanish missions secretly drew traditional Indian symbols on floor tiles and other surfaces of the missions as one means of rebellion.
- The first reservations in California were created in the mid-1800s on military reserves to protect the Native population from the violence of other Californians.

[See Chapter 3: Native Groups in the Northeast for an introduction to the study of major culture areas.]

Early Culture

When Europeans first arrived in California in 1540, the Indian population there was about 310,000 to 340,000 people. These astounding numbers made it the most densely populated area in what is now the United States. The mild climate and abundance of wild foods supported the growth of this large population of California Indians.

Northern coastal tribes fished, hunted sea mammals, and collected food from tidelands. Along rivers and lakes inland, groups hunted, trapped, and fished. Tribes in the central valley, plains, and foothills hunted and gathered wild plants. The greatest variety of food-gathering and economic activities was found in southern California. The Channel Islands (near present-day Los

California (shaded).

Angeles) and nearby coast were rich in sea life. Tribes living along the Colorado River and the area nearby practiced the only agriculture found in aboriginal California.

California Indians organized themselves in a variety of ways. The Yokut in the San Joaquin Valley and the Yuman along the Colorado River are examples of large tribes that shared a common language, owned a well-defined territory, and showed political unity (having reliable, defined relations among people and groups).

A more common way Native California groups organized themselves was in villages, sometimes called tribelets. These villages ranged in size from one to five hundred people. They, too, had well-defined territories.

Several villages were often allied to a large central village where the headman or chief lived.

In both types of social organization, chiefs had limited power. They had ceremonial authority, and were usually wise and influential people who could persuade the community to action. Most chiefs inherited their position. Occasionally groups had female chiefs, but this was not common. Shamans and heads of families also had status and authority.

The traditional tribal areas of the Indians of California.

Native California peoples' view of the world centered around seeking balance in all aspects of life—physical and spiritual. Balance was believed to lead to the well-being of the individual, the extended family, and the tribe. The value of give-and-take, or reciprocity, was important in achieving this balance. In most groups, individuals and villages made offerings to the creator and earth spirits. In return, they expected a favorable relationship between themselves and the natural elements. They hoped for access to game animals, wild foods, favorable winds, sufficient rain, fertility, and so on. This give-and-take principle also formed the basis for economic relationships among individuals, extended families, and neighboring villages.

Each group jealously guarded its territory and resources. Trespassing and poaching (taking resources off another person's land

Spring Rancheria (Cahuilla), c. 1886.

without permission) were serious offenses. They were the principal causes of conflict that would erupt from time to time among the groups.

European Contact

The arrival of Europeans in North America created a clash of profoundly different views of the world. The story of an early encounter in California illustrates this point. In 1579, when English explorer Francis Drake anchored off the California coast, he and his crew came upon the Coast Miwok people, who behaved in very strange ways that the sailors could not understand.

The Coast Miwok viewed the strangers' gifts with fear and refused to accept them.

At the same time, they offered gifts of baskets, food, and ritual objects. The Miwok men showed awe and reverence toward the strangers, but the Native women tore at their cheeks and upper chests, cried and shrieked, and threw themselves on the rocky ground as they walked among the young Englishmen. The English left after five weeks, still baffled by the odd reception they had received.

The mystery of the Indians' peculiar behavior was solved when the Coast Miwok revealed their beliefs. The group believed that the land of the dead lay to the west. The path to that land passed directly beyond the area Drake came from. The young English sailors had sparse beards, just like Native men, and were deeply tanned from years of

Agents of Oppression. Ceramic bowl by Diego Romera depicts Spanish conquistadors and missionaries dominating Native Americans.

sailing on the ocean. The Miwok thought that Drake and his men were dead ancestors. The Miwok refused their gifts because they were strictly forbidden to bring back anything from the land of the dead. The women were simply exhibiting mourning behavior.

Like the Coast Miwok, the English interpreted this meeting with their own misconceptions. The records referred to the headman of the local Indians as a "king," when no such role existed. The English claimed that this "king" gladly surrendered all of "his" territory and authority to the English King, halfway around the world. Finally, the English concluded that the Miwok regarded them as "gods."

Spanish Colonization

Spanish colonization created a catastrophe of huge proportions for the Native peoples of California. In 1769 the Spanish built their first **mission** in the area in the Native village of Cosoy, later called San Diego by the Spanish. With the mission the Spanish planned not only for their Franciscan priests to **convert** Indians to Christianity, but also to reduce the many free and independent Native societies into a mass of slave laborers. They established a chain of 23 missions in California that resembled Caribbean plantations more than churches.

By decree of Spanish law, Indians were baptized. After baptism they were called **neophytes** (or new members) and removed from their villages into areas near the missions. Then they were put to work. Between 1769 and 1836, about 80,000 California Indians were baptized and turned into laborers for the Spanish empire.

At the missions, the Indians were closely controlled. Neophyte children were removed from their families at the age of five or six. They were locked in barracks and watched by colonists who wanted to teach the children without interference from their parents. Indian girls were locked up when they weren't working or attending church. They were freed upon marriage, but if they lost their husbands they were once again locked up in the barracks.

Adults were made to work without pay. Soldiers and **padres** (the priests) whipped, jailed, and punished with additional work any Natives who did not seem to accept Spanish authority. Women and children were not excused from this harsh treatment. One Costanoan Indian neophyte named Lorenzo Asisara reported, "We were always trembling with fear of the lash."

Gabrielino traditional homes, Mission San Gabriel.

Natives Resist

The missions were only supposed to last for ten years, which the Spanish crown felt was long enough to convert the Indians into Christian slaves. In fact, they lasted about 65 years. Many "converts" resisted Spanish rule.

The Natives used three types of resistance to the Spanish tyranny. The most common form was **passive resistance.** Many refused to learn Spanish, or pretended they could not understand commands given in Spanish. Or they would do their work slowly and poorly—a fact that can be seen today in the construction of the old missions. Native laborers secretly drew traditional Indian symbols on floor tiles and other surfaces throughout the missions.

Some Native American women who were sexually assaulted and impregnated by Spanish soldiers practiced abortion or infanticide (killing the newborn baby). They did not want to give birth to children of the enemy, thereby providing a new generation of slave labor for the colonists. From time to time, secret religious activities arose. These were sometimes used to reverse baptisms.

Running away was another alternative. However, Spanish law allowed the Franciscans to pursue runaways. The padres kept detailed records of baptized Indians at each village, and squads of soldiers were stationed

Ramona Lugu, Cahuilla, at her home.

at each mission to patrol the area. Escape was made more difficult because Native tradition forbade anyone who didn't belong to a village from seeking refuge there. Worse yet, if any villager took in a runaway, they risked being assaulted or being taken hostage by the Spanish. Villagers also feared catching deadly diseases that the runaway might bring from the mission. Disastrous epidemic diseases swept through the population of mission Indians, killing many and weakening others. Thousands of Native people fled, in spite of the difficulty. But only about 10 percent (or eight thousand) actually escaped.

Fighting Spanish control was a third form of resistance. Guerilla warfare took place as ex-neophytes like Pomponio of the Coast Miwok and Estanislao of the Yokut organized raids. These raids were directed against the mission, presidio (military posts), and even the civilian herds of cattle, horses, and sheep.

Mission Indians sometimes poisoned the padres; the poisoning deaths of two have been recorded. In 1882, the Indians at Mission Santa Cruz smothered and castrated a padre there who had announced that on the following Sunday he would make use of a terrifying new torture instrument of his own invention. In 1836, Cahuilla Indians kidnapped the padre at Mission San Gabriel and horsewhipped him—just as so many of them had been whipped.

Uprisings by mission Indians were spectacular, and several occurred. The earliest occurred at Mission San Diego in 1775 when one thousand Kumeyaay warriors sacked and burned the mission and killed the padre. In 1781, the Quechan Indians destroyed two missions built in their territory the previous year. In that rebellion, they killed 55 colonists, including 4 padres, 31 soldiers, and 20 civilians.

The last large-scale revolt by mission Indians occurred in 1824. After 30 years of oppression, neophytes from three missions arose to protect their lives and regain their lost freedom. After taking over one mission for more than a month, most were persuaded to surrender after a cannon assault by Spanish troops. However, a number refused to return to the missions. They issued this defiant message to authorities who demanded their return: "We shall maintain ourselves with what God will provide for us in the open country. Moreover, we are soldiers, stone-masons, carpenters, etc., and we will provide for ourselves by our work."

Devastating epidemics were responsible for destroying the majority of Native California peoples in contact with the Spanish colonists. A series of deadly diseases swept through the mission Indian population from 1777 to 1833. When the missions finally collapsed in 1836, about one hundred thousand Indians had died.

After the Missions

After the Mexican Republic was created in 1820, the padres were no longer able to force Indians into labor. As Indians left the missions they found a greatly changed land. Many tribesmen were deprived of their lands and were forced into debt. Many escaped to their former lands in the interior, but found that the landscape had changed greatly. The horses, mules, sheep, pigs, and goats introduced onto the land had ravaged the delicate grasses. The animals continued to multiply in alarming numbers. Mission farming squeezed out native plants. California Indians were not able to live off the land in the way they had before the Spanish came.

Some tribes and villages had virtually disappeared from the face of the earth. So much had been lost that previous forms of leadership no longer existed. New leaders arose, taking much more power and authority for themselves than had been allowed before in any California Native society. Some of these leaders adapted by leading hunts in which half-wild horses and mules were captured. Stock raiding became widespread as well. One spectacular raid in 1840 involved the theft of more than three thousand horses from California ranches.

The Gold Rush and White Settlers

The Gold Rush of 1848 brought more change, especially to Indians living in the interior of California who had not had much contact with the Spanish. Early in the Gold Rush, a few Indians were employed by miners or mined gold on their own. Soon Indians found themselves hunted like wild game by violent and aggressive immigrants.

A series of state laws passed in the mid-1850s virtually enslaved Indians and practically made it legal to kidnap Indian children as laborers. At about the same time, the federal government was negotiating treaties with

Sensioni Cibimoat, basket maker from Warner's Ranch, 1903.

California Indians that would give them 7.5 million acres of land in exchange for the rest of the state's lands. A flood of protests from non-Native Californians occurred because they feared the treaty lands might contain gold. As a result, the U.S. Senate failed to ratify the treaties and they were defeated.

Early reservations, beginning in 1851, were created on military reserves to protect the Native population from the violence of U.S. citizens. In reality, the government reserves served fewer than two thousand Indians at any given time. The vast majority of California Indians survived the best they could on their own. They withdrew into remote areas in their attempt to avoid con-

tact with settlers, but violence against them continued. Casual murder of individuals, vigilante raids, and even occasional army massacres took place.

Some Indian groups continued to fight. For example, the Hupa Indians successfully fought back until 1864, when they were granted a reservation of their own—now the largest in the state. The last and largest war against the California Indians was fought against the Modoc Indians. Under the leadership of Captain Jack, 50 Modoc warriors and their families held off an army of over three thousand for nearly a year. In the end, Jack and three others surrendered and were hanged. Captain Jack and Schochin John were decapitated following their deaths, and their heads eventually wound up in the Smithsonian Institution, in Washington, D.C.

The Ghost Dance Movement

By 1870, a new religious movement, the Ghost Dance, swept west from Nevada. It predicted the end of the world and promised the return of dead relatives and game animals. This vision was especially appealing to Indians at that time, offering a sense of comfort and a focus on the old ways of life. With all the death, disease, and violence the Indians had experienced in the past decades, it probably did seem like the world was ending—in fact, the Indian world, as they had known it, was ending.

The Ghost Dance movement developed a new class of spiritual leaders called dreamer doctors. The movement lasted about two years in California, but it continued to exist in other areas for more than 20 years.

The Twentieth Century

By 1900, after 130 years of foreign domination, less than 18,000 California Indians survived. The staggering loss of almost 95 percent of their people left the survivors deeply demoralized. Hunger, poverty, homelessness, unemployment, and discrimination were widespread. In the midst of this, a number of Native leaders emerged to work toward improving their communities.

California citizens organized several groups to assist Indian peoples. One, the Sequoya League, helped the Kupa to settle in a new place called Pala. Other groups helped Indians such as the Pomo and Win-tun to secure small reservations called rancherias in northern California.

Indian children in California, as in other areas, were shipped off to government boarding schools in the late 1800s for the purpose of assimilation (becoming part of the mainstream society). One of the results was that they met many other Indian children from different tribes. Out of these relationships grew a sense of identity as Indians—not just as members of their own tribes. This sense of identity is sometimes called a **pan-tribal** consciousness (or, awareness of all tribes). This new awareness gave birth to **pan-Indian** (or all-Indian) reform groups. The first such group to include California Indians was the Mission Indian Federation (MIF), founded in 1919. The MIF worked for more independence for tribal governments, full civil rights for Indians, water rights, opposition to the Dawes Act, and the elimination of the Bureau of Indian Affairs.

The first all-Indian reform group formed in northern California was the California Indian Brotherhood. This group sought rancherias for homeless Indians and worked to help move Indian children into public schools with free lunches and clothing. They also sought college opportunities for Indian youth.

Treaty Rights and Land Claims

The problems confronting California Indians in the 1900s varied from community to community. Yet in a way they were not different from the problems confronting other Indian tribes across the country. One issue that all Indians shared in common was the issue of broken federal treaties of 1851-52. A sense of injustice endured. Since Indi-

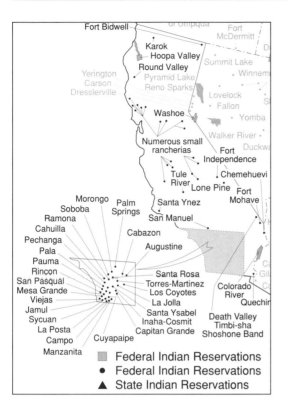

Fort Bidwell
Karok
Hoopa Valley
Round Valley
Yerington
Carson
Dresslerville
Pyramid Lake
Reno Sparks
Summit Lake
Winnem
Lovelock
Fallon
Yomba
Washoe
Numerous small
rancherias
Fort
Independence
Duckwa
Walker River
Tule
River
Lone Pine
Chemehuevi
Fort
Mohave
Morongo
Soboba
Ramona
Cahuilla
Pechanga
Pala
Pauma
Rincon
San Pasqual
Mesa Grande
Viejas
Jamul
Sycuan
La Posta
Campo
Manzanita
Palm
Springs
Santa Ynez
San Manuel
Cabazon
Augustine
Santa Rosa
Torres-Martinez
Los Coyotes
La Jolla
Santa Ysabel
Inaha-Cosmit
Capitan Grande
Cuyapaipe
Colorado
River
Quechir
Death Valley
Timbi-sha
Shoshone Band

☐ Federal Indian Reservations
● Federal Indian Reservations
▲ State Indian Reservations

Contemporary California Indian tribes.

ans did not have the right to vote until 1924, they had no way to pressure public officials for help.

For more than 50 years, reform groups and tribes worked to have their rights restored. The first settlement came in 1944, and paid $150 to every California Indian who could prove they were related to an Indian alive in 1850. In 1968, the second settlement resulted in payment of $.47 an acre for lands outside treaty areas that were lost. Although less than $800 was paid per person, few desperately poor Indians could afford to refuse the money, although they knew it was an unfair settlement.

Civil Rights

The national Civil Rights movement of the 1960s presented new opportunities for Native people to draw attention to the problems and issues facing them. Some of the civil rights achievements California Indians have accomplished since the 1960s include: San Francisco State University becoming the first college to establish a Native American Studies program; the California Rural Indian Health Board being established in 1968 to restore health services in rural and reservation communities; and legal help to seek land, water, and civil rights being made available through the U.S. government's War on Poverty during the 1970s.

Native peoples in California occupied land and buildings as a form of protest over their own lost lands. These activities started a national trend. One of the early occupations, the 1969 occupation of the prison on Alcatraz Island in the San Francisco Bay, was reported in news media around the world! [Also see Activism chapter.]

Return of Burial Objects

In the 1970s and 1980s, millions of new homes and businesses were constructed in California. As a result, thousands of California Indian burial sites and tribal areas were dug up. Anthropologists wanted to remove Indian skeletons and burial objects to laboratories and museums for study. Native American groups protested, demanding to know why only Indian remains are moved about.

At about this same time, Native Americans discovered that the skull of nationally known Modoc war leader Captain Jack had been placed in the Smithsonian Institution.

Outrage over this, and the public display or withholding of thousands of other Indian skeletons, led to a national program. Recent federal laws in 1990 require that all federally funded museums return Indian remains to their tribes of origin.

Cultural Revival

Indian education centers throughout California offer Native language, culture, and dance classes. The first tribally controlled museum was established on the Morongo Indian reservation in 1964. Several publications were begun around this time, including the *Journal of California Anthropology* and *News from Native California*. The California Indian Conference is an annual event, established in 1984 to bring together experts and Native traditionalists to share their interests and knowledge.

In 1993, about 200,000 California Indians lived in the state. As many as 60,000 live on reservations and rancherias and the rest live in nearby towns and cities.

12

Canada's Native Peoples and Their Lands

Major Culture Areas

Culture Groups in Canada

The division between Canada and the United States was put in place by Europeans thousands of years after Native North American groups had settled. Because many Native groups are spread throughout areas within both countries, traditional culture areas have not recognized the border imposed by Westerners. But because contemporary history has so powerfully affected Native Americans, this chapter will consider Canada's **aboriginal** peoples separately from those of the United States.

The history of Canada's aboriginal peoples differs in many ways from the history of the Native peoples of the United States. Early Canadian Native groups were smaller than, and not as interconnected as, U.S. groups, and Canada's settlement by European powers did not take the same course as the settlement of the United States.

The main Western powers in Canada's history were the French and the British. The French fur traders were the first major continuing European presence in Canada. The fur trade was the major factor in the French attitude toward Native groups in the 1600s and 1700s. The French interest was primarily economic—they profited a great deal from the furs the Indians could deliver. The French, who did not acknowledge Indian rights to hold land, had never negotiated in treaty-making with Canadian Indians. Relations between the French and aboriginal peoples of Canada varied from open hostility to shared purpose and friendliness, but throughout their history, the French and the aboriginal Canadians treated each other as separate, sovereign nations. The French never took title to aboriginal lands in Canada.

The British had interests in Canada as well. In particular, the English trading house the Hudson's Bay Company established many trading bases in various areas of Canada and carried on prosperous trade relations with many Indian nations. In 1763, in the Treaty of Paris, the British won almost all French territory in Canada. The British Royal Proclamation of 1763 recognized that North American Indians owned the land in all British territories outside established colonies. The Crown claimed the right to negotiate land surrender and peace treaties with the Indians and prohibited settlement in areas not covered by such treaties.

Canada began to form its own government in 1867 when New Brunswick and Nova Scotia joined with Quebec as a confederation; other **provinces** joined the confederation through the rest of the century.

Unlike U.S. groups, most Canadian aboriginal groups did not engage in drawn-out battles with the Canadian government. In fact, after the American Revolution, many dissatisfied U.S. native groups moved to Canada to escape the oppression they faced at home. By the mid- to late 1800s, however, the Canadian government, like the U.S. government, had placed many restrictions upon Canada's First Nations, denying rights to self-government and rejecting their land claims. Assimilation policies (policies that tried to force aboriginal peoples to become more like mainstream society in Canada) were also imposed.

Canada's Native groups became organized on both national and provincial levels during the second half of the twentieth century. Gaining political representation through their efforts, they won a major battle in 1982 when Canada constitutionally recognized aboriginal peoples. The Constitution Act, 1982, officially divides Canada's aboriginal nations into three designations: the Indian, the Inuit, and the Métis peoples. Today these groups prefer to be known as "First Nations," since their ancestors were the first known inhabitants of present-day Canada.

This chapter is somewhat different than the chapters on major cultural areas of the United States because of the officially recognized grouping of Canada's First Nations. This chapter is divided into three main sections—one for each of the traditional cultural designations of Canada's aboriginal people: Indians, Inuit, and Métis. The group designated as Indian includes **bands** or tribes discussed in the previous chapters—the Algonkian of Eastern Canada and the Iroquois of the Eastern Great Lakes, Plains, Plateau, and Northwest Coast—as well as the Athapaskan of Canada's Western Subarctic region.

Languages

Aboriginal peoples in Canada speak about 50 different languages. These 50 languages can be grouped into 11 language families (groups of related languages). Algonkian and Athapaskan are the two largest language families in Canada.

Most of the aboriginal languages of Canada have been at risk of being lost for many years. Only three—Cree, Ojibway, and Inukitut—are spoken over large areas today. In light of this, many aboriginal communities are trying to preserve native languages by having language and culture programs in their schools. As a result, a considerable number of aboriginal children are learning native languages.

Indians

Indians form the largest and most varied group of Canada's aboriginal peoples. At the end of 1991, over 510,000 Indians were legally recognized by the Canadian government. They are represented at the national level by the Assembly of First Nations. The Indians of Canada are a very diverse group, with many differences in language, culture, and history.

The Algonkian of Eastern Canada

Nations who speak languages in the Algonkian language family occupy a large area of eastern and central Canada. One group of Algonkian-speaking bands live in the woodlands and northern forests of Canada. This group includes the Ojibway and their relatives around the Great Lakes, the Cree of northern Ontario and Quebec, the Innu (Naskapi and Montagnais) of Labrador,

---

WORDS TO KNOW

aboriginal: native; the first or earliest group living in a particular area. When a group of people is called *aboriginal* it is generally being defined in contrast to colonizers or invaders of the land the group occupies. In Canada in the 1990s, the term *aboriginal* is commonly used to describe Native peoples.

band: A Canadian term which originally meant a social and economic group of nomadic hunting peoples. Since Canada's confederation, however, the term means a community of Indians registered under the Indian Act.

province: a district or division of a country. Canada is divided into ten *provinces* and two territories. The *provinces* are: Alberta, British Columbia, Manitoba, New Brunswick, Newfoundland, Nova Scotia, Ontario, Prince Edward Island, Quebec, and Saskatchewan. The two territories are: Northwest Territories and Yukon Territory.

reserve: an area of land set aside for aboriginal peoples to live in, forming a political unit; a Canadian term that corresponds to the U.S. term *reservation*.

tundra: plains in the arctic and subarctic regions that consist of a mucky soil on top of a permanently frozen subsoil. Plant life in the *tundra* is usually limited to mosses, lichen, and small shrubs.

---

and the Micmac and Maliseet of the Maritime Provinces.

Algonkian of Eastern Canada (shaded).

The various woodlands Algonkian groups shared many ways of life in the past. They usually lived in small bands and moved about often. In southern areas, these bands gathered in larger numbers at certain seasons. Most societies were egalitarian, meaning they shared power equally among the members and no one person was extremely powerful. However, some groups like the Micmac did rank their members, giving some higher status and more power than others.

Because the Algonkian people moved about often, their housing was simple and portable. The structures in which they lived came to be known by the Algonkian word *wigwam*. Birchbark provided the ideal cover for wigwams, although moose or caribou hide was used in the north. The covers could

be rolled up and carried between camps, then quickly stretched over a dome-shaped framework of poles. Birchbark also provided lightweight cover for the canoes that were used for travel in the summer. For winter travel, snowshoes were used.

The Algonkian peoples believed they should show respect for the animals they hunted. In their view, the hunter's skill was not enough—the animal had to offer itself to the hunter to be killed. Only by performing ceremonies properly would nature cooperate and give them what they needed to survive. After large game was killed, feasts were held to celebrate and honor the animal. Care was taken with the bones so the animal spirits would not be offended and thus avoid the hunters in the future. Animal skulls were hung from trees, and special platforms were built to keep them out of the reach of dogs. Rituals were performed to discover where game was located, or to learn if anything would be caught during the hunt.

All Algonkian groups had shamans. Shamans were spiritual leaders who could cure diseases or foretell the future. A common ritual was the "shaking tent." Here the violent movements of a small shelter announced the arrival of spirits to assist the shaman in his work.

The Micmac

The Micmac (or Mi'kmaq) occupied the Maritime Provinces, Atlantic Quebec, and southern Newfoundland. The Maliseet, closely related to the Micmac, lived farther inland, along the St. John River valley in western New Brunswick.

The Micmac lived near the coast during warm weather. Coastal areas provided fish,

Ojibway camp on Lake Huron, 1845. Painting by Paul Kane from his travels in the 1840s.

shellfish, and other seafoods such as lobster, sea birds and their eggs, and seals. The Micmac used bark-covered canoes for fishing. In winter they moved inland, where they hunted animals such as beaver and moose. To move about on the deep snow of the interior, they used toboggans (a word that came to English directly from the Micmac).

The Ojibway

The Ojibway (or Ojibwa) are sometimes known in the United States as the Chippewa. They are a collection of groups who originally lived in the western Great Lakes area. They expanded rapidly during the era of fur trade and came to occupy a vast area.

The Ojibway lived in small, independent bands, including the Saulteaux, Ottawa, Nipissing, and Mississauga. They did not consider themselves part of one large group. However, their languages were similar enough that they understood each other, and they held common traditions.

The Ojibway groups lived by hunting, fishing, and gathering plants. Larger groups met seasonally at good fishing locations, such as the rapids at Sault Sainte Marie on Lake Superior. The shallow lakes of the area provided wild rice, an important part of the Ojibway diet. Maple sugar was used as a seasoning for a wide range of foods. Some of the southern groups farmed or traded fish and furs for farm produce.

European Contact and the Beothuk

The arrival of Europeans caused major

changes in aboriginal life. The first Canadian group to encounter Europeans were the Beothuk, who lived on the island of Newfoundland. The group became extinct as a result of European contact.

The Beothuk collected shellfish and hunted both sea and land animals. Bark-covered canoes allowed them to travel out into the stormy north Atlantic to harpoon seals and collect bird's eggs from offshore islands. During the colder months the Beothuk moved inland to the forests to hunt caribou. By building long wooden barriers, they channeled the caribou herds into enclosed areas in which hunters waited with spears or bows and arrows. During these caribou hunts, enough meat was taken to last through several winters.

The Europeans who first contacted the Beothuk gave them the name "Red Indians" because the Beothuk liked to paint their bodies with red ochre (a red-colored clay) and grease. Later the name was applied to other North American Indians, giving rise to the term "Redskins."

As more Europeans settled along the coast, the Beothuk were forced into the interior of the island. Warfare with Europeans, along with European diseases, reduced the Beothuk to a small group. They lived near the center of the island, poorly fed and ill with tuberculosis (a lung disease). In 1829 Shanawdithit, the last of the Beothuk, died, and the Beothuk passed into extinction.

The Fur Trade

When French explorer Jacques Cartier first encountered the Micmac in 1534, they were waving furs and hailing the ship. They were signaling their desire to trade! Appar-

ently, other traders had been there earlier. Iron knives and hatchets, copper kettles, blankets, and other European goods soon replaced hand-made objects among the aboriginal people. In 1630 a French writer noted that the Indians of the St. Lawrence River had already given up traditional clothing for European clothes, and copper kettles had completely replaced vessels of bark.

As trading posts were established in the area, more Native groups came to depend on the fur trade. Instead of hunting for food, they began hunting for furs. Instead of making goods, they bought them. They began to trade for—and eat—European foods, which were less healthy than traditional native foods. Alcohol quickly became popular, and its use frequently disrupted Native societies.

Many Cree and Ojibway tied their fortunes to the fur trade. They spread rapidly to the north and west in search of beaver and other fur-bearing animals. Their occupation of large areas today is a result of the fur trade. Also, their interaction with traders produced a new people, the Métis.

Algonkian Groups Today

Today Algonkian groups are scattered in small **reserves** across a large part of Canada. Hunting, fishing, and trapping are still important means of support, especially in the north. However, environmental problems make it difficult to continue living off the land. Flooding from hydroelectric projects, pollution, and noise from low-flying jets that scatter the caribou herds make hunting difficult or impossible in many areas.

Although many Algonkian groups signed historic treaties, no treaties were signed in Quebec and Labrador. The Cree and Naskapi

Iroquoian of the Eastern Great Lakes (shaded).

of northern Quebec signed the first land claims agreements in modern Canadian history in the 1970s. Other groups continue to press their claims for land and rights.

The Iroquoian of the Eastern Great Lakes

Iroquoian peoples have lived in Canada since prehistoric times. Among Canada's Iroquoian groups are the Huron, Petun, and Neutral in Ontario, and other Iroquoian groups that live along the St. Lawrence River. Today, however, most of the Iroquois in Canada are members of the Six Nations or the League of the Iroquois. Many of these groups came to Canada from New York state after the American Revolution.

The Iroquoian were the only Canadian aboriginal group who farmed, growing corn,

beans, and squash. They also hunted and fished. A common meal was a thick corn soup to which pieces of fish, meat, or squash might be added for variety. They also grew tobacco. In fact, the Jesuits called the Petun the "Tobacco Nation."

Iroquois villages were large collections of longhouses. Some communities had several thousand inhabitants. The bark-covered longhouses sheltered a number of families and were sometimes made longer to house additional people. Raised benches or sleeping platforms ran the length of each side, leaving a central area for cooking fires. Fish and corn, as well as personal belongings, hung from the roof of the house or were buried in covered pits. Many villages were surrounded with palisades of poles twisted into the ground, often in several rows, indicating that warfare was enough of a daily threat to require defense systems. Usually the villages had to move every 10 to 15 years when the soil and supply of firewood were exhausted.

Contact with Europeans

The Iroquoian of the St. Lawrence River were among the first Canadian groups to encounter Europeans. French sailor and explorer Jacques Cartier sailed up the St. Lawrence in 1535, spending the winter near the village of Stadacona (now Quebec City). Cartier recorded few details of his visit there, but left a more complete record of his visit to Hochelaga, near present-day Montreal. Hochelaga was built well back from the river, beyond extensive fields of corn, for protection against intruders. There, Cartier found about 50 longhouses surrounded by three rows of palisades. The palisades had ladders leading up to platforms, where defenders could stand during an attack.

By the time French trader Samuel de Champlain arrived in 1603, Stadacona and Hochelaga had vanished. Only war parties of Algonkian and Mohawk remained. They were locked in bitter conflict over control of the St. Lawrence—an important trade route.

The Ontario Iroquoian

The Ontario Iroquoian, the Huron, Petun, and Neutral, survived into the mid-1600s. All three groups were confederacies (or groups) of separate tribes linked by a common council. Villages were run by local councils: one council in charge of feasts, ceremonies, and other peaceful activities; the other dedicated to matters of war. Councils allowed everyone present to give their opinion. An effort was always made to reach agreement among the members before a decision was formed.

The groups within these confederacies celebrated feasts, dances, and games together. Lacrosse was often played by teams from different villages. It was a popular sport, although it was played so roughly that it could result in injuries.

The most important ceremony was the Feast of the Dead, held every ten years or so. At this time the remains of all who had died since the last Feast of the Dead were removed from their temporary graves. They were reburied in a common pit, with feasting and rituals to honor them.

Warfare shaped much of Iroquoian life. Before contact with Europeans, wars were fought for revenge and to achieve personal status. Later the Iroquoian fought over access to fur-bearing animals and trade routes. Trophies of enemies who were killed were taken back to the villages. Captured enemies were also taken back, and some were incorporated into the society. This was an important method of replacing individuals lost in battle. Other captives were tortured to death in public spectacles.

The Ontario Iroquoian were greatly weakened by infectious diseases brought by the Europeans, but it was warfare that destroyed them. They were overwhelmed by the League of the Iroquois, especially the Seneca and Mohawk, between 1648 and 1651. Many were killed, and others were driven away and lost their tribal identity. The League Iroquois also took captives and "adopted" them into their society.

Warfare caused the Jesuits to flee from their base among the Huron in 1650. The missionaries took along several hundred Huron survivors. Their descendants survive today as the Huron of Lorette (or Nation Huronne Wendat)—a French-speaking community of several thousand people in Quebec.

League of the Iroquois

The great majority of Iroquoian people in Canada today are Iroquois proper, members of the famous League of the Iroquois. These are the Seneca, Cayuga, Onondaga, Oneida, and Mohawk. In the early 1700s one more Iroquoian group, the Tuscarora, joined the league. Since then the league has been called the Six Nations.

The first League Iroquois to move into Canada were converts to Catholicism. They settled on the St. Lawrence in the late 1600s. The largest wave of Iroquois, however, settled in Canada after the American Revolution.

During the war the Mohawk had been loyal to the British. Afterwards, the British rewarded the Mohawk for their loyalty by giving them lands in Canada. Members of all six Iroquois nations, along with Delaware and others who had lost their homelands in the United States, sought refuge in Canada. Each group established separate tribal villages along the Grand River. Today this area is home to the largest Native community in Canada—the Six Nations of the Grand River.

In the 1840s, several hundred Oneida arrived in southern Ontario. They had lost their lands and wished to unite with other members of the league. Today they are known as the Oneidas of the Thames.

At present there are more Iroquois living in Canada than in the United States. Three of the four largest reserve communities in Canada are Iroquois. Of all the Iroquois groups, the Mohawk are the largest. The Mohawk language is considered to have the best chance to survive because the Mohawk insist on running their own educational programs.

Sovereignty

The Iroquois consider themselves to be a sovereign people. They entered Canada with their own governments—the councils within the League of the Iroquois. The Canadian government, however, treats the Iroquois as dependents. Iroquois traditionalists recognize only their traditional councils as governing bodies. This has led to numerous clashes with the governments of Canada and the United States. In 1990 one such clash erupted into violence, with a 78-day standoff between the Canadian army and the Mohawk at Kanesa-

Canadian Plains (shaded).

take, west of Montreal. The Mohawk were resisting expansion of a city golf course onto lands they considered theirs. The situation was eventually defused, but the underlying issues are still not resolved. It did, however, focus attention on Native grievances across Canada. [Also see section on Iroquois in Native Groups of the Northeast chapter.]

Indians of the Plains

The Canadian Plains are made up of the flat, semi-arid grasslands of southern portions of Alberta, Saskatchewan, and Manitoba. Vast herds of bison once roamed across this open land, supplying Plains peoples with meat for food and hides for shelter and clothing.

A Blackfoot on horseback, with a rifle. Artwork by Karl Bodmer, 1833-34.

Throughout the centuries before European contact, Plains people traveled and hunted on foot, using dogs to help carry their goods. Horses brought by the Spanish were used in the southern Plains by the mid-1600s, but they did not become common among Canadian Plains groups until a century later. Starting in the mid-1700s, horses changed Canadian Plains societies greatly. The societies had greater mobility, formed larger social groupings, and produced more elaborate goods. Trade and warfare increased as a result.

Several groups lived on the Plains. Speakers of Algonkian languages dominated the northern Plains. In the west were members of the Blackfoot Confederacy, composed of Blackfoot, Blood, and Peigan. A small group, the Sarcee, joined the Blackfoot Confederacy. Their enemies were the Plains Cree and the Assiniboine and the Plains Ojibway, who came from the woodlands to the east.

All Plains groups based their lives on the vast herds of bison. With the arrival of the horse, hunters could ride along with the stampeding herd, select the animal with care, and kill it with a bow and arrow. Hunting methods that had been used for thousands of years also continued. These were communal (or group) hunting methods where large

An Indian village on the move. Artwork by Charles M. Russell, 1905.

numbers of bison could be taken. They included jumps, where bison were driven over the edge of a cliff, and pounds, where bison were driven into a corral or natural trap. Communal hunting methods required a lot of preparation. Long drive lines had to be built to funnel the animals into the desired location. The cliffs at Head-Smashed-In in southern Alberta are probably the most famous of these sites. They were used for about six thousand years.

The teepee and travois were essential to the mobile life of the Plains. A cover of bison hides sewn together was put over a framework of poles to form the cone-shaped teepee. Flaps at the top helped control smoke from the central fire. An inside liner protected people from drafts. Sleeping robes were laid around the walls and served as couches during the day. When the camp was ready to move, teepees could be taken down quickly. The cover was packed with other belongings on a travois, a framework of poles that was dragged behind a dog, or later a horse.

Warfare, a major part of the Plains culture, was the main way young men acquired status or prestige. Wars ranged from a few individuals setting out to steal horses, to large parties of allied groups engaged in full-scale war. Warrior societies kept order in camp and on the hunt. These societies also provided a common bond linking the various bands into larger associations.

Religion was part of everyday life. The Canadian Plains groups believed that supernatural power could reside in any unusual object or feature of the landscape. Young people sought help from the spirits by fasting and praying in isolated places, hoping for a vision. This was called the vision quest. Medicine bundles, which contained sacred items, were very important ritual objects. Opening a medicine bundle or giving it to a new owner required elaborate ceremonies. Each sacred object was reverently displayed while prayers and songs were recited. Important religious events, such as the Sun Dance, a sacrificial ceremony for the well-being of the community, brought together large numbers of people.

Disease introduced by Europeans, along with the destruction of the bison, weakened Plains cultures. Many Plains people died of smallpox and other diseases during the 1700s and 1800s. Wanton slaughter of the bison and use of the land by European farmers caused the herds to disappear by the early 1880s. With the populations reduced and the bison gone, Plains people were in no position to resist offers of government help in exchange for their lands. Between 1871 and 1877, Canadian Plains tribes signed treaties and gave up claim to much of their land.

In exchange for their lands, Plains peoples were assigned to reserves and given small payments of money and farm equipment. Farming was often a failure. Hunger and disease were widespread. Traditional customs and beliefs, such as the Sun Dance, were discouraged or forbidden.

Refugees from American battles moved into Canada at this time. The Dakota (or Sioux) arrived in two waves. The Santee Dakota fled Minnesota after their uprising was defeated in 1862. The Teton Dakota and their famed chief Sitting Bull sought refuge after devastating Colonel George Custer's army at the Battle of the Little Bighorn. Thousands of Teton Dakota, including Sitting Bull, arrived in Saskatchewan in 1876 and 1877.

By this time, however, the bison were nearly gone and the other Plains Natives were increasingly confined to reserves. The Teton were denied land and rations, and most were forced to leave. Today most Dakota in Canada are Santee, although one Teton community remains. These groups were eventually assigned reserves, and are now considered Canadian Indians without treaty.

Today many reserve communities, particularly in Manitoba and Saskatchewan, lack adequate means of support. Many aboriginals move to the cities as a result. Regina, in the province of Saskatchewan, and Winnipeg, Manitoba, are among the Canadian cities with the highest percentage of Native people.

The Plateau

The Plateau lies between the Rocky Mountains on the east and the Coast Mountains on the west. The environment varies from sagebrush-covered near-desert in the west to heavily forested mountain slopes on the edge of the Rockies. The Canadian Plateau is in southern British Columbia.

Three Native language families are found in this area. The largest is Interior Salish,

Canadian Plateau (shaded).

in large nets, or they could be harpooned or taken in traps. Large quantities of salmon were cut into thin strips and dried in the warm canyon breezes. Salmon was preserved for use in the long winter months and traded with groups who lacked this vital resource. Large groups of people settled around fishing areas because they provided plenty of food. As a result, some areas of the Plateau had very high population densities (a lot of people living close together).

During the winter Plateau people usually lived in pit houses, which were partly underground for insulation against the cold. A log structure was built over a circular pit and covered with bark and earth. Winter villages consisted of a small cluster of pit houses, each sheltering several families. Some groups did not build pit houses. Instead of building below ground they banked snow and earth against their mat-covered lodges to insulate against the cold.

During the warmer months people left the villages for camps near fishing, hunting, root-picking, or berry-picking areas. There they lived in simple shelters made up of bark or mats stretched over a framework of poles.

Each winter village was independent, having several leaders or "chiefs." These chiefs were generally men respected for their abilities in speech-making, hunting, or in war. Shamans were spiritual leaders with the power to cure illnesses. Everyone was expected to find spirit power, setting out at puberty to seek a guardian spirit through the vision quest.

with four languages: Lillooet, Thompson, Okanagan, and Shuswap. The Kutenai in southeastern British Columbia have a language that apparently belongs to no language family. The Plateau Athapaskan consist of the now-extinct Nicola, the Chilcotin, and several groups of southern Carrier.

Interior Salish and Athapaskan

The early Interior Salish and Athapaskcan groups had a way of life based on hunting, fishing, and gathering plant foods. They moved with the seasons as foods became available. They spent much of the late summer and fall catching salmon on their spawning runs upriver. In the canyons, masses of fish could easily be scooped out of the water

The Kutenai

The Kutenai (Kootenay) were different from other Plateau groups. Their language is unlike any other and belongs to no language family. In many ways, their culture resembles those of Plains people. In fact, their first known encounters with Europeans took place on the Plains of southern Alberta.

The Kutenai are divided into Upper and Lower divisions. The Upper Kutenai, who lived near the Rockies and the Plains, hunted big game such as elk, deer, caribou, and mountain goats and sheep in their homelands. They crossed the mountains several times a year to hunt bison on the Plains, which brought them into conflict with the Blackfoot. The Upper Kutenai lived all year long in Plains-style teepees covered with bison hide.

The Lower Kutenai lived farther down the Kootenay River and along Kootenay Lake. In winter they lived in long lodges covered with mats; in warmer months they lived in mat-covered teepees.

Both Upper and Lower Kutenai wore clothing made from tanned hides, typical of Plains and Plateau peoples. In later times, Plains-style feather headdresses were common among the Kutenai.

European Contact

The Plateau Indians' first contact with Europeans came in 1793, as Scottish explorer Sir Alexander Mackenzie traveled through Shuswap and Chilcotin lands on his way to the Pacific. In 1808, Canadian fur trader and explorer Simon Fraser navigated the Fraser River on an expedition to establish trade routes. Among the Plateau Salish, Fraser noticed copper kettles and other European goods that had been traded in from the coast.

Native cultures were not greatly disrupted by settlers until the gold rush in 1858, when thousands of gold-seekers flooded into the area, displacing the Native people from their homelands. Smallpox and other diseases greatly reduced their numbers. During the 1870s and 1880s, they were assigned to small, scattered reserves.

The Plateau groups never ceded their land through treaties. Today land claims are major issues, along with grievances about restrictions on Native fisheries. Plateau peoples fight for resolution of these issues at the provincial and national levels.

The Athapaskan of the Western Subarctic

Members of bands who spoke Athapascan languages occupied much of northwestern North America, from the west side of Hudson Bay to interior Alaska. More than 20 Athapascan languages, closely related and similar to one another, are spoken in the area, which includes Alaska. Many Athapascan groups, particularly those in the north, refer to themselves as the Dene.

Forest covers the Western Subarctic area, which is crossed by numerous rivers and dotted with lakes. Caribou and moose were among the most important game animals for the Athapascans. Bison were also hunted in the southern areas, and mountain goats and sheep were hunted in the Cordillera mountains. Smaller animals, such as the snowshoe hare, were also important food sources. At certain times of the year, great numbers of waterfowl could be caught. The lakes and rivers provided whitefish, lake trout, grayling, and other fish. Groups in the west-

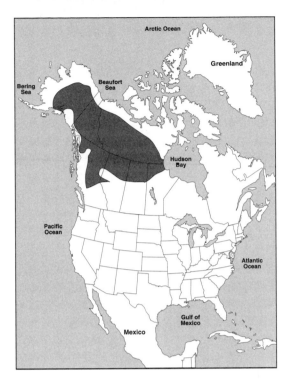

Athapaskan of the Western Subarctic (shaded).

ern areas, where rivers flow to the Pacific, had access to bountiful runs of salmon.

Athapascan societies were generally small. They moved around a lot, following game across a large area. In general, population density was low. Groups did not usually have formal chiefs, although certain people often took leadership roles for specific tasks, such as hunting, trade, or war. Social relations were flexible, and personal freedom was highly valued.

Snowshoes, sleds, and toboggans were essential to winter travel. In summer, people traveled along the lakes and rivers in bark-covered canoes. Housing differed among Athapascan groups, but most used simple hide-covered structures shaped like cones or domes. More substantial winter houses were used in a few areas. In the Yukon, for example, the Han built rectangular pit houses that were heavily banked with earth to withstand the cold.

Athapascan cultures differed with the environment. Three examples can be seen in the Chipewyan, the Beaver, and the Tahltan.

The Chipewyan

The Chipewyan, the largest and most widespread group of the Subarctic Athapascan, lived in the east. During the winter they lived in the northern forest, and during the summer they followed the caribou herds far out into the **tundra** or barrenlands. One of the Chipewyan hunting methods was to drive caribou herds into large circular enclosures made of brush, where they could kill as many animals as they needed. Caribou meat was dried for use in the winter. The hides were made into clothing and lodge covers; they were also cut into strips for snares, nets, and snowshoe laces. The antlers and bones were used for making tools, and the sinew for sewing clothing. Fish was the second most important food source.

The Beaver

The Beaver lived farther south in the Peace River region of northern Alberta and British Columbia. The Beaver lifestyle was based on hunting big game, such as moose and woods bison. They also caught beaver and other smaller animals. Bison herds were occasionally driven into pounds, similar to the way the Plains people hunted them. The

Dene girl at Blanchford Lake Lodge Springs Camp. Quinzees buildings and snowshoes.

Beaver fished only when the search for game failed.

The Tahltan

The Tahltan live in the mountains of the Cordillera. Salmon is at the center of their economy, provided by the salmon runs on the Stikine River. In the past, the Tahltan were in contact with the Tlingit, who lived downriver. As a result, they adopted many features of Northwest Coast culture such as potlatching and matrilineal clans. Because of their location, the Tahltan became middlemen in the trade between the Tlingit on the coast and the Athapascan farther inland.

The Fur Trade

The fur trade with Europeans brought major changes to the Western Subarctic. Trading posts were established on western Hudson Bay as early as 1682. Initially, the trade was controlled by the Cree. The Cree were well-supplied with guns and other European-made goods. This Cree advantage in warfare caused heavy losses of life and land among the Chipewyan. In order to be able to trade with the Chipewyan, the Hudson's Bay Company built Fort Churchill in 1717, after negotiating a peace with the Cree. But the Chipewyan were not as eager

Tabitha Bernard makes traditional Dene bannock at her tent camp. Fort McPherson, Northwest Territory, 1988.

to adopt the fur-trading lifestyle as much as the Cree. Only a few of the groups abandoned their caribou hunts and moved south to find furbearing animals to trade.

Throughout the 1800s, many Athapascan groups focused their economies on trapping animals for furs. Metal tools and European clothing replaced traditional goods; guns and ammunition had become essential trade items.

The Caribou gold rush reached its height in 1862, bringing masses of gold-seekers into the territory of the Carrier. This gravely effected the Cordilleran Athapascans. The 1898 Klondike gold rush had a great impact on the Yukon Athapascan, and nearly destroyed the Han.

Increased non-Indian settlement in the northwest led the Canadian government to make treaties with the Athapascan. Two large treaties cover much of their land. Only the western groups in the Yukon and the Cordillera of British Columbia remain outside of treaty.

Today Athapascan communities in northern Canada rely on a combination of trapping, wage labor, and government assistance. Local trapping and hunting are threatened by non-Native commercial development and settlement. Groups such as the

Inuit Areas (shaded).

Inuit woman on a snowmobile.

Dene Nation in the Northwest Territories are fighting for the right to self-determination and to resolve Native land claims.

The Inuit

The Inuit were formerly known as Eskimo, a Cree word meaning "raw meat eaters" that is rarely used in Canada today. They are the native occupants of the Arctic. The Inuit are different from other aboriginal Canadians in terms of both their cultural and their physical characteristics. In fact, the Inuit are more closely related to Siberian peoples than to other aboriginal groups. It is believed that the ancestors of the Inuit were the last peoples to cross the Bering Sea Land Bridge that connected Siberia and present-day Alaska, perhaps about 10,000 years ago.

The Inuit speak a single language, Inukitut. They are represented at the national level by a council called the Inuit Tapirisat of Canada. Because the Inuit are not registered by the Canadian government, their exact population is not known. However, there are believed to be about 30,000 Inuit in Canada.

The Inuit live in the Canadian Arctic—lands lying north of the tree line that border on the Arctic Ocean. The lands of the Arctic are varied. There are rugged mountains and fjords (narrow sea inlets between cliffs) on the eastern islands, rocky lands in the interior, and flat plains on the Mackenzie Delta. Because the Arctic is so far north winters are long and extremely cold. In the northern regions there is a period of time every winter when the sun never comes out; it is night 24

Annie Kilabuk and Iga Ishulutak at "Qittaq Qamarq" women's sewing group, stretching sealskin in a village in Northwest Territory.

hours a day. Summers are short and moderate in temperature, with long daylight hours.

Prior to European contact, Inukitut, the Inuit language, was spoken across the entire Canadian Arctic. Population density was low and social groups were usually small. However, tasks during certain seasons, such as winter seal or whale hunting, brought together larger numbers of people. Leadership was generally informal (there were no official chiefs). The opinion of the most experienced and respected elder usually carried the greatest weight in group decisions.

All groups relied on hunting land and sea animals, along with fishing. Caribou and seals were the primary food sources,

although walrus and whales were hunted by some groups. Because plant life was scarce, gathering played a minor role in the Arctic economy. Delicacies such as berries and birds' eggs were gathered when possible in season.

Caribou were important as food, but also for their hides. The hides were taken in fall when they were in the best condition, and used to make winter clothing. For the Inuit, winter clothing consisted of two layers of coats, pants, stockings, and boots; the inner layer of clothing placed the fur of the animal hide next to the wearer's skin for warmth. Summer clothing was a single layer and was often made of sealskin. Sealskin

Inuit hunters in the Canadian North.

boots were also essential for wet conditions. Women's clothing was often more elaborate than men's, with extra space at the back for carrying babies against the mother's skin. Clothing style and decoration varied among the regions.

The Inuit believed that success in finding food depended on observing strict taboos (rules forbidding people to do certain things). One of the most common taboos was the belief that products of land and sea must not be mixed. For example, seal and caribou meat were never cooked together. Also, all sewing of caribou skins for winter clothing had to be completed before the people moved to their sealing camps on the sea ice. Inuit Shamans had powers that enabled them to cure the sick, foresee the future, and locate game animals.

The Inuit of the Mackenzie Delta region lived in the West, and were closely related to Inuit groups in northern Alaska. Whaling

was an important part of their economy. The large bowhead whale was hunted on the Beaufort Sea from umiaks (large, hide-covered open boats). These Inuit also hunted small beluga whales from their kayaks in the shallow waters of the delta.

The Mackenzie Delta Inuit had the densest concentration of Inuit people in Canada. Their homes, in large villages along the delta, were log houses built of driftwood and partly covered by earth. Infectious diseases nearly wiped out this group by the end of the 1800s. Since then, the population has been replaced by people coming from Alaska. Today this Inuit group refers to itself as the Inuvialuit.

In the central Arctic are the Copper, Netsilik, Iglulik, and Baffinland Inuit. In the winter most groups have traditionally moved far out onto the sea ice. There they hunted seals by finding the breathing holes the animals make in the ice and waiting for their prey to surface. During this time they lived in dome-shaped snow houses, or igloos. These igloos were lighted and heated with lamps made of soapstone; the lamps use whale blubber (fat) as fuel. In summer and fall people lived inland in tents made of sealskin, and they fished and hunted.

The Caribou Inuit, who are closely related to the Mackenzie Delta Inuit, live on the interior lands west of Hudson Bay. They have traditionally relied almost totally on hunting caribou. Depending on a single resource in this way is dangerous, and periods of starvation occurred.

In the east were various Inuit groups of northern Quebec and Labrador. They hunted sea mammals, including walrus, seals, and whales. The Inuit harpooned these ani-

Inuit street scene, Repulse Bay.

mals from kayaks or umiaks in summer, and from the edge of the ice in the winter. Caribou and fish were also important.

European Contact

The Inuit first encountered Europeans in the tenth century, when the Norse (Norwegians) settled Greenland. The Inuit of the eastern Canadian Arctic were also in contact with the Norse, at least briefly. Shortly after 1500, fisherman and whalers of several European nations traveling the waters off the Labrador coast probably came upon Inuit groups.

For most of the Canadian Arctic, however, sustained contact did not begin until the late 1800s with the arrival of European and U.S. whalers. At that time, European goods became commonplace, and diseases brought in by settlers drastically reduced Inuit populations. The Sadlermiut of Hudson Bay became extinct. The Inuit of the Mackenzie Delta were reduced to a small remnant population. After the whaling industry collapsed around 1910, European presence was limited to a small number of trading posts, police posts, and missions.

World War II brought large numbers of military personnel into the Arctic. After World War II, the Canadian government took a more active role in the area. Schools and medical stations were built, and housing programs were established. The Inuit were encouraged to move out of their hunting camps and relocate in settlements.

The Inuit Today

The Inuit Tapirisat of Canada is the national political organization formed to promote Inuit culture and identity and to provide a common front on political and economic issues. Canadian Inuit also participate in the Inuit Circumpolar Conference, an international organization bringing together Inuit from Greenland, Canada, Alaska, and Siberia to strengthen pan-Inuit communication and cultural activities, and to promote international cooperation in protecting the Arctic environment.

Land claims have been a major part of modern Inuit political struggles. The Canadian government made settlements with the Inuit of northern Quebec in 1975 and the Inuvialuit of the western Arctic in 1984.

Canada is made up of ten provinces and two territories, of which the Northwest Territories is one. In a large section of the Northwest Territories the Inuit have sought to establish a self-governing homeland to be known as Nunavut, meaning "Our Land" in Inuktitut. Nunavut is to have the status of a province, and will have an Inuit majority. A tentative agreement has already been reached between the Inuit and the Canadian government to divide the Northwest Territories. Nunavut is expected to become a reality in the not-too-distant future.

MÉTIS

The Métis, unlike the Indians and Inuit, emerged as a group in Canada only after

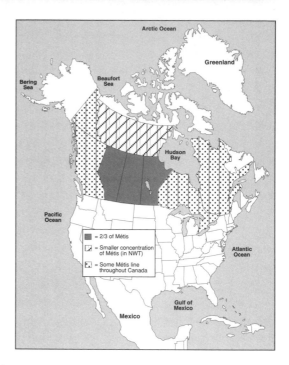

Métis Areas.

European contact. The group was originally comprised of the offspring of marriages between French-Canadian fur traders and Native women, mostly Cree. The Métis take their name from an old French word meaning "mixed," and have at times been called the "children of the fur trade."

During the 1800s the Métis created a distinct identity and culture on the Canadian Plains, combining European and Indian traditions. They attempted to form a Métis nation in the Canadian West, but their efforts to win legal recognition as a separate group were defeated in 1885. At that time it was expected that they would blend in with the rest of the Canadian population. This did not happen. At present controversy continues about how the Métis should be

Métis bison hunt near Fort Garry in 1846. Painting by Paul Kane from his travels in the 1840s.

defined or how many of them exist today. They are represented nationally by the Métis National Council.

As the fur trade moved westward, many French-speaking men married Cree and Ojibway women. Aside from the usual reasons for marriage, the traders benefitted from these marriages in their work. Trade was made easier by having relationships with the Native people. Native women acted as interpreters. They also performed skilled tasks such as making snowshoes, drying meat, and dressing furs. Male children of these marriages often became traders, and a distinct group of people with mixed heritage began to emerge.

To the north, English and Scottish employees of the Hudson's Bay Company married Cree women, in spite of company rules against such marriages. In the early years of contact, these traders usually returned to Britain at the end of their service, leaving their wives and children at the forts.

By the mid-1700s, a large "mixed blood" population had settled around the Great Lakes. Fairly large communities of log cabins emerged at Sault Sainte Marie and other locations. As fur-bearing animals became scarce and settlers moved in from the east, many of these mixed-blood Native people moved westward to the Plains, where the distinctive Métis culture emerged.

The center of Métis culture formed at the point where the Red and Assiniboine rivers joined (near present-day Winnipeg, Manitoba). There they established themselves as buffalo hunters and suppliers for the North West Company.

The Métis conducted communal bison hunts, which provided food and brought the smaller groups together to form structures with the larger group. Large parties would set out on the hunt in their two-wheeled Red River carts pulled by horses or oxen. Once the hunters located herds, they killed the bison from horseback. The meat was cut into strips, dried, pounded into coarse powder, mixed with melted fat, and sewn into hide bags. This was called pemmican, an important part of the fur trade economy. Pemmican was an important winter food for many of the trading posts of the distant Northwest.

By the 1850s, the bison herds were disappearing and Métis hunters were forced to move farther and farther out. Many began to spend their winters on the Plains. Soon, more permanent Métis settlements moved to the Plains.

Europeans began encroaching on Métis lands, and in 1869 the Hudson's Bay Company sold the Métis homelands to Canada. A group of Métis, led by activist leader Louis Riel, Jr., challenged the local government of the Manitoba territory by forming their own government. The Métis arrested several people for resisting Métis law and executed one of them, causing an uproar. The Canadian government negotiated with the Métis and met some of their demands for allotments of land.

As Métis groups moved westward in pursuit of buffalo, there was continued conflict with other Canadian settlers. In 1884 the Métis of Saskatchewan sent for Louis Riel. He petitioned the government for land title and provincial status for Saskatchewan,

LOUIS RIEL,
CHEF MÉTIS,
Exécuté le 16 Novembre 1885,
MARTYR POLITIQUE !
Coupable d'avoir aimé ses compatriotes opprimés,
Victime du fanatisme orangiste, auquel l'ont sacrifié des politiciens sans âme et sans cœur.

QUE LES VRAIS PATRIOTES S'EN SOUVIENNENT !!

Louis Riel's execution in 1885 raised him to the status of martyr for the Métis cause. He remains one of the most controversial figure in Canadian history.

Assiniboine, and Alberta. When the government failed to satisfy Métis demands, Riel set up another provisional government. Armed conflicts followed. Riel, who had become a national hero among the Métis, was captured, put on trial, and hanged for treason in 1885.

After Riel's death the Canadian government made some concessions to the Métis. The Manitoba Métis, for example, were given 1.4 million acres of land. In exchange, they gave up all claim to other Canadian lands. However, because of fraud, many

Métis never received the lands they were promised. Others sold their lands to get money to live on. By the twentieth century, many were living in poverty.

The demands that Riel and other Métis activists made upon Canada have not been forgotten in the century since his death. Prior to 1982, the Métis had argued for many years that they were entitled to aboriginal rights. When the Métis were included in the definition of aboriginal people in Canada's 1982 Constitution, many considered it a major victory. They still battle for equal recognition with Inuit and Indians as one of Canada's three aboriginal groups.

During the 1960s provincial Métis organizations sprang up in Manitoba, Alberta, and British Columbia. In 1970 the Western Métis formed the Native Council of Canada (NCC) to represent the Métis and other non-status Indians. The NCC has taken a "pan-Canadian" approach, defining the Métis as any people of mixed European and Indian blood. However, in the 1980s, it faced a challenge from the prairie Métis, who define the Métis as a particular national group that arose in the Métis homeland during the development of the fur trade.

The different provinces in which the Métis now live have dealt with the groups in different manners. Alberta, in particular, has established "settlements" in the northern part of the province for Métis groups. But while the political organization of Métis groups has been effective in gaining land and rights in some provinces, the Métis in many areas have experienced troubled relations with other aboriginal groups and with the government, which, despite the 1982 act, does not treat them quite the same as it treats other aboriginals.

13
Urbanization

Native Americans Move to the Cities

FACT FOCUS

- In 1990, 22 percent of Native Americans lived on reservations. Less than half of Canada's aboriginal people live on reserves.
- In the 1950s, U.S. government officials decided to try to make Indians assimilate, or "blend in" with the rest of society, rather than keeping their own distinct cultures. This policy meant moving Indians from reservations to cities, where the government hoped Indians would find work and adopt an "American" lifestyle.
- Children on reservations enjoy better health than Indian children in the cities, who are more likely to get pneumonia, the flu, and lung disease.
- In Canada there are urban reserves that look very similar to the city neighborhoods around them.

Non-Reservation Indians in the United States

Native peoples in the United States have survived five hundred years of conquest, defeat, genocide (the murder of large numbers of people), and disease. Native Americans have always fought for the land of their ancestors and, most of the time, they have been forced off the land by the conquering Europeans. As one Indian wise man said: "The White Man never kept his word, except once when he said he wanted our land, and he took it."

In the beginning, reservations were set up as "holding pens" for conquered peoples.

Gradually, they were seen as a way to get rid of Indian populations and take over their lands. But after succeeding in confining tribes to reservations, the government decided it would attempt to do away with reservations altogether by encouraging Indians to move to cities and towns and "blend" with non-Indian people. Since resources and educational opportunities were limited within the reservations, many Indians left for urban areas to seek work and skills not otherwise available to them.

Although Indian tribes of North America lost much of their land to the conquerors, they won the right to exist as separate, self-governing nations within the United States and Canada. The system of reservation life that was imposed on them by these governments isolated them for many years from non-Indian society. Thus, although uprooted, often impoverished, and forced to learn European-based languages, religions, and traditions, reservation Indian tribes have remained in separate communities, isolated from mainstream American society. Perhaps more than other groups, they have maintained separate traditions, values, and culture.

When Native Americans move in increasing numbers to North American cities, some tribal leaders fear that the tribal cultures will be disrupted. They fear that in leaving the communities that exist on reservations, **urban** Indians may lose their sense of Indian identity, along with their native language, values, and traditions. Other leaders, however, believe that Indians in American cities can preserve their differences while availing themselves, and often their tribes, of advantages necessary to their welfare.

According to the 1990 **census** (a government count of people), only 22 percent of the Native population lives on reservations. There are believed to be at least 10 million people in the United States who have Indian blood, but are unaware of it. These are "invisible" Indians who appear to be of white, Hispanic, or other ethnic origins.

Early Urbanization

Ever since Europeans first appeared in North America, Native Americans have been interacting with the newcomers' society. Many early scouts, sailors, guides, craftsmen, and farmers were "urban Indians." They left their tribal homes and went

---

WORDS TO KNOW

census: an official count of the people in an area. A *census* is usually taken by the government, and includes information such as the number of people living in a house or apartment, their age, sex, occupation, and other facts.

general assistance: help, usually in the form of money, given by the government to people who are unable to support themselves.

urban: having to do with cities and towns. The opposite of *urban* is rural (having to do with the countryside). An *urban* Indian is one who lives in cities or the areas around them.

urbanization: the process of moving from a rural to an urban environment, or from the country to the city. In many cases in this chapter, *urbanization* refers to Native Americans moving off reservations to live in the city.

---

to work with settlers and traders in European centers. **Urbanization** (moving to the cities) is not really a new process!

Actually, urbanization began centuries ago. Long before Europeans arrived in the Western Hemisphere, the Native peoples had developed urban centers of their own. In central Mexico, for example, urban areas existed thousands of years ago. When the Europeans arrived, the largest city in the Americas, Tenochtitlán, had a population of over 150,000 people!

The peoples of North America also built

and lived in large urban centers. Moundville, in present-day Alabama, and Pueblo Bonito, in present-day New Mexico, had several thousand people each. It is believed that 40,000 people lived in the ancient city of Cahokia (near present-day St. Louis, Missouri) as late as A.D. 1200.

Urbanization since 1930

Throughout history, many Native Americans have moved to towns, but in the past 40 years their numbers are rapidly increasing. In 1930, less than 10 percent lived in a city. In 1970, 45 percent of Native Americans lived in cities. By 1990, this figure had risen to 66 percent. Much of this movement has resulted from specific U.S. government policies.

In the 1950s, the U.S. government decided to end the "Indian problem" once and for all. Government officials decided to try to make Indians assimilate, or "blend in" with the rest of society, rather than keeping their own cultures. This policy meant moving Indians from reservations to cities. The government hoped Indians would find work in the cities and adopt an "American" lifestyle. Then, the government would be able to "terminate" the tribes and get rid of the reservations.

In 1952, the Bureau of Indian Affairs began a program to help Native Americans find jobs off the reservation. In 1956, Congress passed a law that provided job skills training for Native Americans between the ages of 18 and 35. They would be given money to support themselves for six months while they were in training.

The government's Termination Policy began in 1953. Several tribes were terminated, meaning they lost their status and

PERCENTAGE OF NATIVE AMERICANS IN CITIES, 1990	
City	**Percentage**
Tulsa, OK	6.8
Oklahoma City,	4.8
Tucson, AZ	3.0
Phoenix, AZ	1.8
Seattle-Tacoma, WA	1.3
Minneapolis-St. Paul, MN	1.0
San Diego, CA	.8
San Francisco, CA	.7
Los Angeles, CA	.6
New York, NY	.3

power as nations. The Klamath and Menominee are two of the tribes that were terminated. Congress also passed a law that gave states and local governments control over tribal members. These actions took away the tribes' authority to govern themselves.

By 1961, the government began to realize that these policies were causing damage to Native Americans. The government stated that terminating tribes hurt Indian morale and made the Native people angry or apathetic (not willing to make an effort). The statement went on to say that these reactions limited Native Americans' willingness to go along with other federal Indian programs.

Government policies began to change. The Bureau of Indian Affairs has not actively encouraged Indians to move to the cities since the late 1960s. However, many continued to relocate for many of the same reasons

Urban Indians drumming in downtown Los Angeles.

anyone might: to be with family or friends, to find a better job, to get an education, or just to find a different way of life.

The Crisis in Tribal Identity

Today, there are some urban Native Americans who have never seen their reservation. They have never spoken their tribal language, or learned about the history and culture of their people. Many Native American leaders see this as the most important crisis Indians have faced since European contact five hundred years ago. Urbanization has posed a new problem: How can Native Americans keep an Indian identity while living in cities, separated from the rest of their people? In other words, will living in cities lead to the disappearance of many Native American cultures?

Native American leaders are concerned about these issues for a number of reasons. It is common for people living in cities to have fewer children than people living in rural areas. Now that most Indians live in the cities, the Native American birth rate will be lower. If the population levels off, Native peoples will form a small sub-group in the United States. As an even smaller group, it is feared that Native Americans will lose some of their power and influence, and there will be fewer people to carry on Native American traditions and culture.

Some Native American leaders are also concerned about the high rate at which Indi-

Los Angeles urban Indian center.

ans marry non-Indians in the cities. In 1980, over half of all Native Americans were married to non-Indians. Today the rate is even higher. Eventually it may be hard to even define Native Americans as a group. It is expected that by the year 2080, only 8 percent of Native Americans will be more than half Indian by blood.

Tribal leaders have also expressed concern that many urban Indians no longer consider themselves members of a tribe. The 1980 census showed that nearly 25 percent of Native Americans did not feel that they belonged to a tribe. Also, more Native Americans are learning English as their first language than ever before. This adds to the loss of connection with the tribe.

On the other hand, not all Native leaders agree that urbanization will lead to the loss of tribal culture. They feel that:

1) Native Americans, unlike other minority groups, are native to the land in which they live. They may have been moved from their ancestral lands, but they still have a significant land base within the United States and Canada. Therefore, they retain a tie to their homelands even if they live in the city.

2) Native Americans still think their own cultural values are better than American values.

3) Many Native Americans have not really blended in with American society. Racism has excluded many people of color from the mainstream. Since many Indians feel they are outside the mainstream, they are not as likely to give up the old values.

4) Many Native Americans continue to value the sacred, traditional Indian ways of life. They wish to preserve these for the benefit of all Americans.

Indian college students from the American Indian studies program, University of California, Los Angeles, sell fry bread on Bruin Walk.

The Quality of Life for Urban Native Americans

When Native Americans move to the city they face many challenges. One of these is the conflict between tribal values and the values of American society. Children, especially, may have difficulty in finding their place.

Urban Native Americans are often forced to meet their needs without much money. Rent, child care, transportation, and health care are all available on the reservation. However, they may be difficult or impossible to find in the city. In 1980, about 25 percent of urban Indians lived in poverty. One study showed that only about 2 percent manage to get **general assistance** (money

from the government) to help with living expenses. Native Americans who have spent their lives on reservations often do not know how to apply for general assistance. Sometimes the people working in government agencies refuse aid to Native Americans, mistakenly thinking that Indians are already receiving help from the Bureau of Indian Affairs.

Lack of education is one cause of low income and unemployment. Over 40 percent of urban Indian teenagers drop out of high school. Non-Indians are twice as likely to have a college education as Indians. For Indians, as with other groups, lack of education often means working low-income jobs that do not provide health insurance. Many Indians cannot find health care in the cities; the Indian Health Service only serves Native Americans who live on reservations.

In fact, Indian health is better on the reservations than in American cities. Native American children in cities get more pneumonia, flu, and lung disease than those on reservations. More die as infants in cities than on reservations. Many of these children have health problems because their mothers did not receive proper care when they were pregnant. For adults, the main health problems are accidents, heart and liver diseases, cancer, suicide, alcoholism, and diabetes.

In the cities of the Midwest and the West, poor Indians often live in ghettos (neighborhoods in cities in which members of a particular minority group live). Their households are often crowded because many live with family or friends when they can't afford to pay rent. Many do not have telephones or transportation. These problems of urban poverty combine to make a very poor quality of life for many Indians in the city, although they usually lose the financial assistance provided on reservations.

Urban Native Americans and the Federal Government

If Native Americans move to cities, they do not lose their status as Indians. As citizens of Indian tribes, Native Americans keep their special rights and privileges. The federal government has had a *trust* relationship with Native Americans since the late 1700s and early 1800s. This means that the government must act to protect and preserve Native Americans. No court decision and no act of Congress has ever changed this rela-

tionship, although it has often been disregarded or unfairly interpreted by the government.

The Supreme Court once ruled that federal services are not limited to reservation Indians, but Congress has been very slow to give aid to urban Indians. In fact, it was not until 1967 that Congress gave any money for urban Indian programs. And that was only for one program in South Dakota!

For several years after 1967, very little money was actually given to urban Indian programs. At this time, however, urban Indians were beginning to organize to help each other. At first they started small volunteer clinics. These clinics provided community support and helped Native Americans with problems such as lack of housing, jobs, and health care. Urban Indians started programs to maintain cultural traditions as well. Most of these programs were funded by small grants and were only able to serve Indian people in limited areas.

In 1976 Congress passed a law to help urban Indians. This law was called the Indian Health Care Improvement Act. By the late 1980s, $9.6 million was given to urban programs. These funds helped more than half a million urban Indians. Even though this is a start, the money is not enough to help the number of Native Americans who need services.

Conclusion

Native Americans in the United States have moved to the cities for many reasons. While some have returned to the reservations, most remain in urban areas. Those who stay are faced with unique challenges. Many have found ways to combine the old traditions and cultures with new lifestyles. More and more, Indians in the city are making an effort to keep their Indian identity. Native Americans have persevered against tremendous odds for hundreds of years and they continue to persevere.

Along with all the problems it has brought with it, urbanization has led to many positive things. There is a current Native American rebirth of spirit. Much of this has come from the activities of Indians in the city. For example, the takeover of Alcatraz in San Francisco was started by urban Indians. The radical political group AIM (American Indian Movement) was started in Minneapolis, Minnesota. [Also see Activism chapter.]

Many leaders on the reservations are former urban Indians who have returned to share valuable skills they learned while off the reservation. Many Native American scholars, university professors, artists, and leaders acquired skills in the cities. Urban Indians who have succeeded in mainstream society frequently continue to serve Indian people. They do this in spite of pressures to "blend in" with non-Indians.

Canadian Urbanization

Less than half the aboriginal (native) people in Canada live on reserves (the Canadian term for reservations). Most leave the reserves to look for better jobs and education in the cities. Reserves are relatively small places that cannot always provide the kinds of opportunities found in major cities. Aboriginal people, like people from other groups, move to cities to share in the social and cultural opportunities they find there. As populations on the reserves increase, shortages in housing, jobs, and other necessities occur. A move to the city may seem very attractive under these conditions.

Most aboriginal people in Canada move to the city without having made a decision to stay permanently. This is somewhat different than the way most non-aboriginals move. Especially in western Canada, Indians tend to move between the city and reserve quite often. But some Canadian Indians make a permanent move off the reservation. In the cities there are more and more aboriginal people who were born there, or who have grown up there. Very recently, Inuit have been moving from the far North to southern cities. They have also been moving to some of the larger cities in the North.

A Variety of Settings

A majority of the urban aboriginal people in Canada are poor. They are either unemployed or work in low-paying jobs with little security. Many of the poorest households are headed by single mothers. Many households include extended family, such as uncles, cousins, in-laws, and grandparents. Aboriginal people are imprisoned at many times the rate of non-aboriginal people. Despite the poor circumstances most Indians face in Canada's cities, a substantial group of urban aboriginals in Canada work successfully in business, government, and other professions.

At least 65,000 aboriginal people live in Toronto, which is Canada's largest city. This is the largest number of aboriginal people in any Canadian city. However, the smaller prairie cities, such as Winnipeg, in the province of Manitoba, Calgary, in Alberta,

First annual Vancouver, British Columbia, War Dance Ceremonies, 1970.

and Regina, in Saskatchewan, have larger proportions of aboriginal people. In other words, if these cities were as large as Toronto, they would have more aboriginal people than Toronto.

All Canadian cities and most towns have organizations to serve the urban aboriginal peoples. Some cities also have social service agencies for aboriginal peoples. The Friendship Centres are one example. They provide places for meetings, social events, and fundraising events. They may also deliver a variety of services, including job training, job placement, cultural programs, instruction in aboriginal languages, courses in crafts and marketing, personal counseling, and healing

circles. In a few centers, urban Indians have started political advocacy organizations. These groups represent aboriginal views and needs to local and federal governments.

There are also some urban reserves. Two examples are the Musqueam reserve near Vancouver and the Kahnawake reserve near Montreal. They are small reserves and not very different from the surrounding neighborhoods. These urban reserves are often as wealthy as the cities nearby, or even more so. They have the advantage of not having to pay taxes, which is a right given to Canadian aborginals by treaty. The urban reserves also benefit from being located so close to the larger markets in these cities.

Special Difficulties in Urban Centers

Some aboriginal people who move to the city have the education and skills to find good jobs. They form part of a growing middle and upper class of aboriginals. However, the great majority of urban aboriginal people live in poverty. They live in poor and overcrowded housing and may be discouraged about looking for jobs. Poor diet and health problems are common.

In addition, urban aboriginal people may face racism, which often makes it difficult for them to find housing and jobs. At the same time, many deal with feelings of loneliness because they are no longer in the close community of the reserve. Those who are able to find work often try to help support unemployed relatives.

Another difficulty is that urban aboriginal people in Canada, like those in the United States, do not receive the same services as other poor people in the cities. Until recently neither the federal government nor the provinces and cities have been willing to take responsibility.

The federal government argued that it was not responsible for status Indians who do not live on reserves. Thus, urban Canadian Indians have had trouble for many years getting the benefits that were due to them by treaty. They also have had trouble getting the federal help that is available to all poor Canadians. At the same time, the provinces and cities would not provide services, arguing that this was the federal government's responsibility.

Slowly, change has begun. One reason for this change is that aboriginal peoples have gained power through political struggles. [Also see Activism chapter]. These struggles have made the Canadian people more aware of the rights of aboriginals. As a result, programs in education and social services are being created. The quality of urban aboriginal life is slowly changing, but there is still a long way to go.

There are not many political organizations that represent urban aboriginal peoples. The few that exist are composed of members of several different tribes or First Nations. This suggests that urban aboriginal peoples seek each other out because they are living in the same area and not because they are from the same tribal groups. They are forming new aboriginal communities.

Cooperative housing, the Friendship Centres, and other services and businesses are part of this new development. Not all aboriginal people are willing to "blend in" to the larger Canadian society. Even those who are successful professionals are creating new ways to adapt the urban setting to their special needs as aboriginal people.

14

Law, Treaties, and Land Claims

FACT FOCUS

- Native peoples made treaties with each other long before Europeans arrived. However, these treaties never involved giving away land.
- The Cherokee had a democratic political process in which group decisions were generally made only after hearing the opinion of every tribal member who wanted to speak.
- British law upheld the natural right of Indians to the North American lands they occupied. One reason some colonists argued for independence from England before the Revolutionary War was their desire to acquire more Indian lands than the English king would allow.
- Between 1778 and 1881, the United States and Native nations signed over four hundred treaties.
- Tribes were considered sovereign nations (independent in the same way as other foreign nations) under European law of the 1500s and under the terms of most treaties.
- Native American people were not granted citizenship in the United States until 1924, when they were given the right to vote and be taxed.

Native Law

Each group of Native American peoples had its own system of law before the first Europeans arrived. These **legal systems** included rules about government, property rights, and everyday life.

Some groups, like the southwestern Pueblo and some of the Northwest Coast tribes, ranked their members according to status. They gave the authority for making decisions to certain individuals with high status. These types of societies are called "hierarchical." In contrast, the southeastern Cherokee made group decisions only after listening to every member who wished to speak. An individual was never forced to act on a group decision if he or she didn't agree with it. Groups like this are called "egalitarian." The Iroquois Confederacy is yet anoth-

Proceedings of the Floridians in deliberating on important affairs. Drawing by Le Moyne, from an engraving by Theodore de Bry.

er example of the variety of ways in which Indian peoples governed themselves. The Iroquois developed a complex political system under a constitution called the "Great Law" to join warring tribes together in order to create peace and unity.

Although there were many differences among the Indian tribes, their legal systems shared certain features:

1) Laws were transmitted orally, rather than being written down. However, some Eastern tribes kept records in the form of wampum belts (strings of polished shells).

These served to remind the people of a law or a pledge.

2) Law and religion were considered one system with the same goals.

3) Native law aimed to restore peace and tranquility, while European law concentrated on protection of property and punishment for doing wrong.

In these ways, Native American law is very different from European law. As a result, European explorers and settlers often failed to understand and recognize tribal laws and legal systems.

Treaties

Treaty-making among the Indians

Long before Europeans arrived, Native peoples were making **treaties** among themselves. A treaty usually created family-like relationships between groups. The treaty itself was a simple idea. For example, it might require all members of one tribe to act as brothers toward members of another tribe. This relationship could often be stated in a single word, although its full meaning would grow and change from generation to generation.

Native people never sold land or gave it up through treaties. They viewed the land as a resource to be shared. However, treaties could have economic value. Although land could not be sold, it could be shared with relatives. Joining together as a family—or as "brothers"—allowed tribes to share resources. On the Great Plains, for example, allied tribes freely crossed each other's territory in search of game, often camping and hunting together in the summer. In the Pacific Northwest, related tribes fished together and formed huge trade networks extending from Alaska to California.

Treaty-making usually involved exchanging symbolic gifts, which were meant to remind the parties about their agreement. For example, in the Eastern Woodlands, furs and wampum were used as gifts in the treaty-making process. Certain designs in Algonkian and Iroquoian wampum belts came to have special meanings, similar to the written words in a European treaty.

A religious ceremony was often included in the treaty-making process to express the seriousness of promises made between

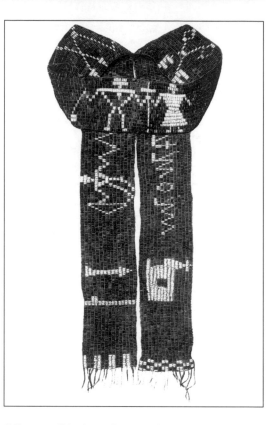

"Wampum" in the collection of the Vatican, Rome, recording a 1610 agreement with the Micmac, made in present-day Nova Scotia.

groups. The tribes of the Ohio and Missouri Rivers used the "calumet" or pipe ceremony for this purpose. The great feasts, or potlatches, of the Pacific Northwest also served to ratify treaties among the chiefs of different clans, villages, and nations.

Native North American nations met frequently to retell the history and meaning of their treaties, to resolve disputes, and to reaffirm promises made in the past. For most Native American groups a treaty was not a single document, but a continuing, living relationship, strengthened over the years through meetings.

European Treaties and Indian Lands

Many of the first relations between European explorers and Native peoples were friendly and respectful, although cautious. Generally, Native peoples welcomed the strangers and wanted to trade with them. The Europeans were faced with a new land that was sometimes harsh and unpredictable, and they needed, and frequently received, help from the Native peoples simply in order to survive. At this early stage, treaties were signed between Europeans and Native peoples to show their mutual respect for each other. European law of the sixteenth century gave native peoples **aboriginal title** to their lands. This meant that they owned the land because they were the first, or original, inhabitants.

The Two Row Wampum is an example of an early treaty in which both parties viewed each other as sovereign, independent nations. The Two Row Wampum was signed between the Iroquois and the Dutch, and later by the British. In this treaty, the Europeans kept their "ship"—an expression meaning that they kept their own laws, government, religious beliefs, and customs. Likewise, the Iroquois kept their "great canoe"—meaning that they would keep their Great Law (similar to our Constitution) and their system of democracy. The Europeans expected to travel down the river of life in their "ship" alongside the Iroquois in their "great canoe." They would share in the bounty of the land and waters, but they agreed not to interfere with each other's ways.

Land Hunger Changes European Attitudes

Unfortunately, the spirit of these early treaties was soon broken. Europeans (especially the British) began to change from friendly partners to aggressive colonizers. As they gained experience and population within the new lands, they began to try to

---

> ### WORDS TO KNOW
>
> **aboriginal title:** the claim of the first inhabitants of an area to title or legal ownership of that area, based on the fact that they lived there first.
>
> **land claim:** a demand for the return of land. For example, a tribe may ask for lands that they or their ancestors once inhabited to be returned to them if they feel the lands were taken away illegally.
>
> **legal system:** a group's laws, and the way they are learned and enforced.
>
> **title:** a statement or document that shows ownership of a piece of property. In the United States and Canada, one must have *title* to a piece of property in order be recognized as the legal owner.
>
> **treaty:** an agreement between two parties or two nations, signed by both, usually defining the benefits to both parties that will result from one side giving up title to a territory of land.
>
> **trust:** a relationship between two parties (or groups), in which one is responsible for acting in the other's best interests. The U.S. government has a *trust* relationship with tribal nations. Many tribes do not own their lands outright; according to treaty, the government owns the land "in trust" and tribes are given the use of it.

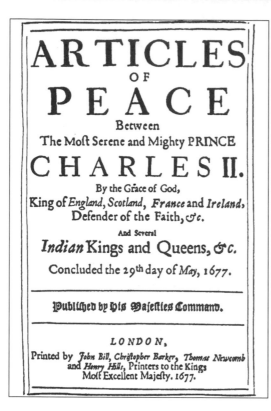

ARTICLES
OF
PEACE
Between
The Moſt Serene and Mighty PRINCE
CHARLES II.
By the Grace of God,
King of *England*, *Scotland*, *France* and *Ireland*,
Defender of the Faith, &c.
And Several
Indian Kings and Queens, &c.

Concluded the 29th day of *May*, 1677.

Publiſhed by his Majeſties Command.

LONDON,
Printed by *John Bill*, *Chriſtopher Barker*, *Thomas Newcomb*
and *Henry Hills*, Printers to the Kings
Moſt Excellent Majeſty. 1677.

The title page of one of the first Indiian treaties to be printed in English, the 1677 Articles of Peace with the Pamunkey and Nottaway of the eastern shores of Virginia.

dominate Native peoples and take their lands. Many of the colonist groups, through traditions of their own, had the idea that they were superior to Indians, whom they viewed as primitive, non-Christian, and lacking in culture. Some colonial groups began to assume that they had the divine right (a right given by God) to control Indian peoples and their lands.

These attitudes were in direct conflict with European law. The British king had repeatedly issued warnings to colonists about settling on Indian lands, but the colonists continued to ignore his instructions. Even George Washington, the first U.S. president, violated this law. Indians protested illegal settlement on their lands, and occasionally engaged in battle over this issue.

The Royal Proclamation of 1763

Finally, King George III of England issued the Royal Proclamation of 1763. This document stated again that Native nations had aboriginal title to their lands, and that only the British Crown—not the colonists—could buy land from them. The Proclamation set limits on the growth of the colonies, directing that lands beyond colonial areas were Indian territory, where Indian peoples were to be left "unmolested." The Proclamation also described the proper way to make treaties and appointed two ambassadors to conduct relations between the British king and Native American leaders.

One of these ambassadors was Sir William Johnson, who established close relations with the Iroquois. Among other actions, Johnson formally read out the Royal Proclamation as if it were a treaty. In this way he assured gatherings of Indian nations at Niagara in 1764, and at Detroit in 1766, that their lands would be protected. Johnson presented wampum belts and medals to represent this "agreement." But in spite of these and other efforts by Johnson, colonists and settlers continued to ignore the Proclamation and take Native American lands. Conflict between settlers and Indians continued.

Conflict among groups of colonists also increased because very often two or more European powers wanted the same Indian lands. To avoid conflict, the colonists developed the "doctrine of discovery." The doc-

The second Fort Laramie Treaty in 1868 brought an end to one Plains Indian war and set the stage for another. Here, Sioux leaders meet with the United States delegation, which includes generals Harney, Sherman, and Terry, and, at the far right holding a ledger, Commissioner of Indian Affairs Taylor.

trine of discovery proclaimed that the first European power to claim a territory had the right to purchase land and settle there. As a result, the English, French, and other colonists became intent on being first to "discover" and claim land. This created a rush of exploration. Unfortunately, the lands they were rushing to explore and settle had been "discovered" long ago by Native peoples and were now their homelands.

Europeans Prefer to Buy Rather than Fight

Usually Europeans preferred to buy land rather than fight for it. Although they found many reasons for fighting battles over land,

prolonged warfare was costly in human life and money. More importantly, Europeans were vastly outnumbered by Indians, and it was expensive to ship large armies across the Atlantic Ocean. Great tribal confederacies controlled the Great Lakes, Ohio Valley, and the Mississippi. War with these nations might cause other European powers to join in the battle. It simply made more sense for the Europeans to claim land by treaty than by fighting.

European Treaties

In contrast to the way American Indian groups made treaties among themselves,

European colonists filled their treaties with military and commercial details. The main goal of most treaties was to acquire land. Europeans viewed treaties as fixed and final documents giving them permanent rights. Most Native groups, on the other hand, viewed treaties as "living documents" that could grow and change over time.

Colonists continued to make treaties with Indians, despite the Royal Proclamation's decree that only the British Crown could do so. Conflict between the colonists and the British king over Indian affairs was actually one of the reasons colonists wanted independence from England. British Americans did not want their westward expansion limited by the king, and this was one of the grievances they listed in the Declaration of Independence.

Treaties between the United States and Native Nations

The New American Government

After the United States gained its independence from England, the newly formed U.S. Congress signed its first treaty with the Delaware Indians in 1778. In 1871, Congress banned any further Indian treaties. During those 93 years the United States made over four hundred treaties with Indian nations. These were ratified (approved) by the Senate in the same way treaties with foreign nations were ratified.

Most treaties with the Indians included the following terms:

1) Indians gave up their land in exchange for a reservation.

2) Tribes remained self-governing (sovereign), but under the "protection" of the United States.

3) Indians were given water, hunting, fishing, and gathering rights on reservations, and sometimes on the lands they gave up as well.

4) The federal government would control matters involving non-Indians who were on, or dealing with, reservations. For example, trade between Indians and non-Indians, or crimes involving both, would be under federal control.

5) The United States would give needed supplies and services to the Indians such as food, health care, and education.

After the United States was formed, states began to compete with the federal government for control over Indian affairs. Both the states and the federal government began to make treaties with the Indians. The Constitution of 1789 attempted to settle the issue by stating that the federal government had authority over dealings with the Indians and that states could no longer negotiate treaties.

The Treaty Era Ends in 1871

Under the U.S. Constitution, treaties were signed by the president and ratified (approved) by two-thirds of the members of the Senate. Congress ended treaty-making in 1871. After 1871, Congress passed legislation (new laws) to manage Indian affairs. Even though the method of dealing with Indians changed, their legal status (or rights under law) remained the same.

After 1871, U.S. presidents made "agreements" with the Indians for the sale of their land, even though treaties were no longer being written. These agreements were basically the same as treaties, except that they did not recognize tribes as independent nations.

"Annuities" being paid to Lake Superior Chippewa in Wisconsin, about 1871. After the Civil War, payments for land under individual treaties were gradually converted into a social-welfare system, through which Indians received services under Federal supervision instead of cash.

Regardless of whether the documents they signed were called treaties or agreements, Native nations lost their lands. In fact, at the end of the treaty era in 1871, American Indian tribes still controlled one-tenth of the 48 states, or about one-fourth of the land between the Mississippi and the Rocky Mountains. By the early 1900s, much of this land would be owned by the U.S. government.

The Native View of Treaties

Starting in the late 1700s and continuing through part of the 1900s, the U.S. government bought over 20 million square miles of Indian land. Most of these purchases were made through treaties and agreements negotiated with tribal groups. At the time, the American public remained, for the most part, unconcerned about fairness of the way lands were passing from Native Americans to the government, and many "sales" were forced upon the tribes.

Although the Indians had a long history of signing treaties among themselves, they had never before considered giving away or selling their land. Territory was owned by a particular nation or shared with neighbors, but it was never given away, and only lost through war. Many American Indian tribes

Five Sauk and Fox and three Kansa flank the U.S. commissioner of Indian Affairs.

did not believe they were giving away all rights to their lands. Often when they signed treaties, they felt they were merely agreeing to share their territory.

Land Claims and the Return of Lands

During the 1960s and 1970s, the civil rights movement produced changes in the public outlook of the United States. The emergence of the Red Power movement and the founding of the American Indian Movement (AIM) influenced the passage of laws that were favorable toward Indians. [Also see Activism chapter.] One result of the activism of the 1960s and 1970s is that some land began to be returned to Indians—a pre-viously unheard of step. Although many **land claims** have not succeeded, some have brought either monetary or land awards to Indian groups.

In 1970 Congress passed a law returning 48,000 acres in New Mexico to the Taos Pueblo. This land included Blue Lake, an area sacred to the community. In 1971 Congress returned 44 million acres and gave $962.5 million to Alaska Natives in exchange for releasing land claims for the rest of Alaska. In the following years, land was returned to other tribes, including the Yakima of Washington state, the Havasupai of Arizona, the Narragansett of Massachusetts, and the Penobscot and Passamaquoddy of Maine.

Status of Indian Treaties Today

The U.S. government has a **trust** responsibility toward American Indians. This means that the government must act in the best interest of Native American peoples. "Best interest" is a term that is open to various interpretations. For example, for many years federal policy maintained that it was in the best interest of Native Americans to be assimilated into—or blend in with—mainstream American society. Many Native Americans did not agree. The trust relationship also means that Native American groups do not own their land outright—their land may not be leased, mortgaged, or transferred without federal as well as tribal approval.

Today, the stated government policy is to interpret Indian treaties in the way the Indians would have understood them at the time they were made. For example, a tribe may not have intended to give up its lands permanently when signing a treaty. If there is any evidence of the tribe's original interpretation of the treaty (what they thought they were getting or giving away), the treaty must be honored under those terms. If the beliefs of the tribe and the U.S. government at the time of treaty-making cannot be determined, then the tribe must be given the benefit of the doubt. In other words, the treaties are to be understood from the Indian point of view.

This current policy recognizes the fact that most tribes were at a great disadvantage when the treaties were signed. Many Native American groups negotiated treaties with the United Stated based on their own separate understanding of law, politics, and values. Many treaties were forced on tribes, and often the parties who signed them were not representative of the group as a whole.

Sergeants Red Tomahawk and Eagle Man, Standing Rock Agency Police.

Legal Status of Native Peoples in the United States

Indian Country

Indian reservations are political communities with special status. According to federal law and the terms of over four hundred treaties, Indian tribes have sovereign power (the power to act as independent nations). Although most Native American governments are based on reservations, sovereignty can extend beyond reservations, by the terms of the definition of "Indian Country." Indian Country is a term used in federal law that includes reservations, scattered Indian homesites, and sometimes areas near reservations as well. By law, tribal governments in Indian Country have the authority to make and enforce their own laws. They also can enter into agreements with the United States, just as any other foreign government can.

Conflicting Laws

Although American Indian nations are sovereign, Native American peoples are also governed by the state, local, and federal laws that govern all Americans. Often these laws conflict with tribal laws or the decisions of the tribal governments. This has often been the case in disputes over fishing rights, when limits set by local governments conflict with Native American communities' treaty rights in regard to fishing. When this occurs, it usually takes a court ruling to decide which authority—the tribe or the local government—has the final say.

Further complications may occur because, in addition, treaties usually promised the Indians special protection and services from the government. Sometimes the government may make a decision to "protect" the tribes, but the tribe may not feel that the decision is in their best interest. The tribe may also feel that the "protection" interferes with their ability to govern themselves as sovereign nations.

To add to the legal complexities, federal and state governments also pass laws that deal only with Native American peoples. Sometimes these special laws conflict with the laws all Americans are expected to follow.

Native Americans Become Citizens

Under the original terms of the U.S. Constitution, tribal Indians could not vote or be taxed. This was because they were viewed as citizens of a foreign nation, not of the United States. By the end of the 1800s, treaty-making ended and the government policy changed to assimilate Indians into society. Non-Indian groups began to promote the idea of citizenship for Indians.

Finally, in 1924 Congress passed a law that gave state and federal citizenship to all Indians. As citizens, Indians are entitled to the same rights under the U.S. Constitution as anyone else. But they also keep the special rights they were granted by treaties and other federal laws.

Termination

In 1953, Congress passed a law that ended (or terminated) the special relationship of trust between the U.S. government and native nations. Under the policy of termination, Indians were to lose their special privileges and be treated just the same as any other U.S. citizens. Starting in 1954, Congress began to terminate tribes. That year Congress terminated the Klamath of southern Oregon; four Paiute bands and the Uintah and Ouray of Utah; and the Alabama and Coushatta of Texas. Over the next few years, other terminations followed.

Termination was devastating for most tribes, who could barely survive as a community even with recognized tribal status. Without the trust relationship and the rights they had been granted by law and treaty, most of these groups faced extreme poverty and the threat of loss of their community.

Navajo Nation Supreme Court associate justice Homer Bluehouse swears in new Navajo police officers during a police cadets graduation ceremony at the Law Enforcement Training Academy at Toyei, Arizona.

The termination of the Menominee of Wisconsin, for example, forced the group to sell valuable lakefront property. They were unable to pay the taxes on it that, as sovereign nations, they had not had to pay in the past. When their reservation lands became a county of Wisconsin, they struggled to keep their lumber operations going. The Menominee, becoming impoverished soon after termination, appealed to Congress to have their treaty rights restored. In the mid-1970s they became the first Indian nation to regain their former status as Indian nations. Several other terminated tribes, including the Siletz of Oregon, were later restored to their original status.

Tribal Governments Exercise Their Sovereignty

Since the 1960s, self-government for Indian tribes has been supported by the U.S. government, and a number of laws have passed that support Indian sovereignty. However, federal and state governments still exert control over reservations because they are considered "guardians" or "trustees" of Indians. The ideas of trust and sovereignty often conflict in a very direct way. Some Native Americans feel this conflict prevents tribes from moving forward.

Native American governments work to maintain their independence as sovereign nations. Tribal governments perform many functions. They define tribal membership, determine how tribal resources will be used, establish rules for everyday life, and resolve disputes. Tribal governments may impose taxes on activities of Indians and non-Indians alike on reservations.

Because they are considered sovereign nations, tribal governments can also try criminals in their own courts, even though the criminal will be tried in a state or federal court for the same crime. Today, tribes usually establish their own rules and issue their own licenses for hunting and fishing on their reservations. These apply to both Indians and non-Indians.

Tribal governments work to reclaim lost homelands and to receive treaty rights. In addition, Indian tribes have demanded that lost Indian skeletal remains, funeral objects, sacred objects, and cultural items be returned. Many such items have been taken by museums, collectors, and scholars. Some states have agreed to return them. Also, the federal government passed a law in 1990 requiring all federally funded museums to return any remains and objects they still have.

Canadian Treaties, Land Claims, and the Legal Status of First Nations

Before the arrival of European settlers, aboriginal groups in Canada had traditions in law similar to Native groups in what is now the United States. The laws reflected religious beliefs and morals that emphasized individual freedom while placing primary importance on the harmony and well-being of the community.

Canada had a different history with European powers than the United States. Up until 1760, Canada was basically a French possession. British rule was confirmed in 1763 by the Treaty of Paris. Britain handed control of Indian affairs to the colonies in 1860. When Nova Scotia, New Brunswick, Quebec, and Ontario joined in a federal union in 1867, Indian affairs were assigned to the central government in Ottawa, Ontario.

France

The French Crown signed no treaties in which land was surrendered by any Indian bands or tribes. New France, the French colonies in Canada, did not require the removal of Indians to make way for settlers, and French settlement of western lands was generally not allowed. Catholic missions, fur trading posts, and military garrisons were established with the permission of local Indians, for whom it was customary to share resources in trade and alliances in war.

When battles erupted between French colonists and Indian groups, the treaties that were signed to make peace did not take away Indian rights or land. In 1760, when Britain became the ruling power in Canada, France took care to protect the rights of the First Nations as it ceded its position in Canada.

Britain

While the British Royal Proclamation of 1763 set out many protective measures for Indian rights to land and sovereignty, it maintained the right of the British Crown to dispose of Indian lands and removed the right of Indian peoples to sell or lease their lands as they chose. For many years Britain's presence in Canada did not threaten most bands' way of life or land rights. But gradually Indian lands were given up through treaties. By 1830 the immigration of increasing numbers of Europeans made the aboriginal lands more appealing to the British. They offered small reserves, annual incomes, medical help, and some training in return for aboriginal groups' giving away large tracts of land. In 1850 the government became even more land-hungry, seeking forest reserves, mineral deposits, and travel routes through Indian lands. After that time, twice as much land as had already been ceded in Upper Canada was lost to Native Canadian groups.

The Robinson-Superior and Robinson-Huron treaties were signed with Indians living in the upper Great Lakes in 1850. These treaties provided a model for later treaties. They involved the surrender of large areas of land. In exchange, the Indian nations were given reserves (reservations), payments of money, and fishing and hunting rights.

The Confederation of Canada

Reserves established by the Canadian government are different from reservations in the United States. First, tribes were not removed from their homelands. Secondly, different tribes were not placed together on the same reservation.

After confederation in 1867, Canada wanted to open lands in the west for settlement and get rid of aboriginal claims to those lands. Between 1871 and 1923 the Canadian government signed 11 treaties that now cover the provinces of Manitoba, Saskatchewan, Alberta, northern Ontario, and the Mackenzie Valley region of the Northwest Territories. These 11 treaties are often referred to as "numbered treaties" because they are titled "Treaty Number 1," "Treaty Number 2," and so on.

In addition to exchanging land for Indian reserves, the numbered treaties typically guaranteed Indian hunting and fishing rights on land that was given up, but which remained unoccupied. Provisions were made for education and agricultural development on the reserves, and included a system of annuities (annual payments to the bands).

However, there is much debate over what these provisions actually mean to the Indians and to the government. For example, some Indian groups claim that a university education is a treaty right. Some feel that the Canadian government should provide complete health care because of the "medicine chest" provision in many treaties. "Medicine chest" clauses stated that the government would provide medical supplies to the reserves.

Some Indian leaders argue that, in general, Native people were misled and cheated during the treaty-making process. Therefore, more lands, rights, and benefits are due to them. These leaders believe that the treaties should be renegotiated.

Land Claims

Many of the lands and other benefits that were promised to Indians by treaty have not been delivered, leading several Indian nations to file land claims. Land claims in Canada fall into two groups—comprehensive and specific. Comprehensive land claims are made when an aboriginal people can show that their rights to the land have not been extinguished (or given up). Aboriginal title to Native lands is supported by King George's Royal Proclamation of 1763. This decree states that aboriginal people still own any land they have not given up by signing a treaty. Many Native groups in Canada are seeking comprehensive claims.

Specific claims involve disputes over particular promises given by treaty. These may involve lands that were not given as promised, or resources such as cattle that were not provided. Some First Nations have claimed that Native lands and assets (resources) have been mismanaged, and therefore the government must repay the band for losses incurred because of this. Numerous specific claims of this type have been filed, and several have been settled.

The Inuit of northern Quebec and the James Bay Cree were involved in the first modern land claims agreement to be reached in Canada. Signed in 1975, this agreement guaranteed hunting and fishing rights over parts of northern Quebec and "ownership" of other parcels of land. It also established the Kativik regional government for the Inuit of the area, rights to education and use of the Inukitut language, and a cash and royalties settlement amounting to $90 million for the Inuit. In return, the Inuit and Cree gave up any claim to other lands.

In a 1991 land claim settlement, the creation of a new territory called "Nunavit" was proposed. It involved 350,000 square kilometers (about 560,000 square miles) of land and a payment to the Inuit of $580 million. In return the Inuit gave up all rights to the rest of their traditional lands. It is expected that the new territory will be created by the end of the twentieth century.

Larry Pierre of the Okanagan on the occasion of the First Nations Constitutional Conference, 1980, demanding Native participation in constitutional tasks.

Legal Status of Aboriginal Peoples

Indians in Canada are divided into three groups: status, treaty, and non-status Indians. These categories affect the benefits or rights Indians are given by the government.

A status Indian is a person who is registered with the government as an Indian. The Indian Act, passed in 1876, first established

Indian chiefs open the first ministers' conference on aboriginal issues, March, 1983. This conference, guaranteed by the 1982 Constitution, marked the first time that aboriginals were given full participation at constitutional conferences.

the category of "status Indian." Status Indians are members of the 633 bands across Canada and as of 1990, there were about 500,000 status Indians in Canada.

A treaty Indian is a person who is a registered member of a band that signed a treaty, or a person who can prove he or she is descended from such a band. Indians living in most of the province of British Columbia are not treaty Indians because the area was not covered by treaty. However, they would still be status Indians.

Non-status Indians are people who are Indian, but who have lost their right to be registered under the Indian Act as a status Indian. In the past, the most common reason for losing the right to be a status Indian has been marriage of a registered Indian to a non-Indian. Another way Indians have become non-status was to have served in one of the world wars. By serving in the military, they were given full citizenship and therefore lost their status as Indians.

The Indian Act was amended (changed) in 1985. At that time, women who had lost their Indian status by marrying non-Indians and their children were able to register as Indians once again. By 1991, about 92,000 Indians had registered to regain their status as Indians.

Self-Determination

Many groups in Canada are seeking greater self-determination. First Nations have filed claims to restore lands and rights (such as fishing and hunting rights). Land claims are one of the major areas of "unfinished business" between Canadian Natives and government. Native people see land claims as a way to assert their aboriginal rights, as well as to gain their economic independence (the ability of a people to support itself with a reasonable standard of living). Economic independence is seen as a key to self-government.

Another way to achieve self-government is by direct negotiation. In 1986 the Sechelt of British Columbia, through negotiating with the Canadian government, received **title** to their reserve lands, the right to draft their own constitution and laws, and various other rights.

Education plays an important role in the drive for both self-government and the preservation of Native culture and languages. Most Canadian bands now run all or part of their educational programs. Three groups (the Nisga'a of British Columbia and the Cree and Inuit of northern Quebec) operate their own school boards.

Federal funding for the college education of Indian and Inuit students has helped to produce many young, educated Native leaders. Through this active leadership and their long struggle, Canada's First Nations continue to take control over their own lives, and ensure the survival of their cultures.

INDEX

Wovoka 101, 199-200
Wyandotte 19

Y

Yakima 29, 100, 104, 106, 162
Yokut 108
Yukon Native Products 229
Yuman 108
Yupik 86, 87, 91

Z

Zuni 15, 29, 64, 180, 294